From Diversity to Unity

From Diversity to Unity

✦

Creating the Energy of Connection

Mary E. Casey and
Geraldine M. Bown

iUniverse, Inc.
New York Lincoln Shanghai

From Diversity to Unity
Creating the Energy of Connection

iUniverse, Inc.

For information address:
iUniverse, Inc.
2021 Pine Lake Road, Suite 100
Lincoln, NE 68512
www.iuniverse.com

ISBN: 0-595-27463-3

Contents

The Authors

Mary Casey is the president and owner of Centerpoint Consulting in Minneapolis, Minnesota. Established in 1992, Centerpoint Consulting provides training, consulting and coaching services that provide cutting-edge strategies for improving productivity and performance.

Mary's background includes working with Fortune 500 companies throughout the United States and Europe. As a trainer and consultant, Mary brings a wealth of experience having developed and implemented leadership and team development programs in such organisations as Land O" Lakes, American Express, 3M, General Mills Dupont Europe, The Welsh Office and many more. As a resident of the United Kingdom for six years, Mary also **experienced first hand the issues of diversity and culture and incorporates a global and multicultural perspective. Mary hold a Master's Degree in training** and organisation development from the University of Minnesota, and is currently an instructor at the University of St. Thomas Management Center in Minneapolis, Minnesota. See www.centerpoint-consulting.com

Geraldine Bown is the founder and Managing Director of The Domino Consultancy Limited, an equality and diversity consultancy, established in 1986 in the UK; a former President of the European Women's Management Development Network; the current Vice-President of the European Institute for Managing Diversity; and the Managing Director of Domino Perspectives Limited. She has spoken at many international conferences and has co-authored three books written for women managers, which are now translated into Chinese, Spanish, Indonesian, German, Bulgarian and Czech.

Gerladine is committed to helping organisations to provide an environment in the workplace for nurturing the spirits of individuals through ceremonies and celebrations, dialogue groups and spiritual counseling. See www.dominoperspectives.co.uk

Personally, Geraldine is a Reiki Master practitioner and in September 1998 was ordained as an InterFaith Minister.

Acknowledgements

We would like to thank some special people who took the time to read a first draft of this book, and provided us with their exceptionally valuable comments and insights: Kathleen Casey, Rose Casey, Karen Elliot, Sondra Hollinger-Samuels, Ray Murray, Jude Smith Rachele, Frances Tolton, Joseph Wheeler. We are very grateful to you all. In addition, we would like to thank our editor, Mary Beth Bossert for her consistent help.

Finally, a big thanks to all the people we have worked with during the many years of our diversity work, who have not only shared their stories and struggles with us, but have also inspired us by showing us what is possible.

Introduction

Humankind has not woven the web of life.
We are but one thread within it.
Whatever we do to the web, we do to ourselves.
All things are bound together.
All things connect.

—*Chief Seattle*

This book provides a new approach to diversity. In this approach, differences and issues of diversity are considered within the framework of unity and connectedness. Individual differences clearly make us unique, and provide the rich texture of our individual experiences, but emphasizing these differences can only take us so far. In moving from diversity to unity, a new framework is created. This new framework is based on unity, and borrows from the field of quantum physics. Quantum physics has demonstrated that underlying all the "perceived" differences in the material world is an unbroken wholeness and a unified field of all possibilities. These findings are aligned with many spiritual principles. Our approach is to develop and present a new set of relationship skills and strategies that incorporate these spiritual principles and build on these new discoveries about reality. Incorporating fundamental principles of unity, connection and wholeness in our communication strategies allows new relationship patterns to emerge. Inherent in all diversity is the potential for misunderstandings, misperceptions and conflicts based on attachment to a particular point of view. By developing relationship skills and strategies that are based on unity, wholeness and connection, a new space is opened that allows for deeper dialogue about differences while it increases the potential for understanding and respect. In this process, diversity is taken to a new level. In our approach, the "business case" or the reasons for dealing effectively with diversity are considered key to this process and are covered in Chapter One.

In *Creating the Energy of Connection*, we don't actually create the energy, for this energy is already there. Instead, individuals learn to tap into the energy of connection, and by doing so discover new relationship patterns that arise out of unity, appreciation, and connectedness. Like water that is transformed into ice, snow or mist, so too can we work with the energy of connection to transform our perceptions and our relationships. By aligning ourselves with principles of unity and shifting our own inner energy, we allow new patterns of openness and understanding to emerge in our relationships with others and in our relationship with ourselves. *Creating the Energy of Connection* is about each individual learning that they have the power to transform their own perceptions while learning a set of corresponding tools that positively impact the dynamics in their relationships—regardless of what the other person is doing.

We understand there is controversy inherent in this point of view. In an early draft of the book, we asked for feedback from a number of friends and colleagues including many people of color. From this feedback we learned that it is possible for someone to interpret our perspective to mean that by asking *everyone* to take responsibility for their perceptions and share the work to create the energy of connection, we are "blaming the victim." This is absolutely not our intention nor is it our point. We understand that reprehensible acts of discrimination, hatred and violence are committed against people with certain differences every day, and we support *eradicating all* such negative actions. Our point is that every day there are also a myriad of communication difficulties and conflicts between diverse individuals in the workplace that never reach effective resolution—let alone a level of sincere understanding. It is our belief that current approaches to developing diversity skills do not provide an adequate framework for individuals to learn to transform diversity issues and conflicts into opportunities for discovery, real learning and meaningful exchanges. When we consider that unity is a fundamental principle of reality, and that we are all connected parts of a larger whole, it follows that each person in a situation contributes equally to the reality that ultimately gets played out. In our approach, each person—regardless of their background or differences—has the opportunity to create new relationship patterns for themselves.

An additional piece of feedback is also important to mention. After reading the first draft, an African American friend commented that, as a woman of color, she already spends tons of energy getting others to overcome their biases towards her. She said it might seem we are asking diverse people—many of whom are already exhausted from trying to get others to overcome their biases towards them—to take on even more. This is not at all what we are suggesting. We completely empathize with the energy it takes to constantly be aware of how others perceive you, and the effort of having to constantly evaluate what, if any, behavioral adjustments you want to make. In our approach, we are simply asking that individuals try some of these unity-based strategies and skills. You can then find out for yourself what kind of energy is involved, and whether this approach is helpful or not.

It is also important to mention, that while a premise of this book is that it only takes one person to shift in the dynamics of a relationship by changing themselves, it is still *always* a legitimate option for either person in a relationship to choose to *not* do the work in that setting, and walk away.

A final word is about language. As co-authors residing in two different countries—Britain and the United States—we could not afford two separate book printings each using the appropriate spellings and word choices for each country. And rather than choose one approach over the other, we decided to intersperse the different spellings and word choices throughout the book thereby offering the reader an opportunity to experience—in real-time—their own cultural preferences, biases and judgments. Pay attention to how "wrong" a perfectly correct spelling in another country looks to you, and what conditioned thoughts are behind your perception. By doing this, you are peeking behind the veil of attachment to your own point of view, and setting the stage to go beyond the limited and the familiar. You are also setting the stage to discover the powerful tools and skills that make up the practice of *Creating the Energy of Connection.*

1

Moving from Diversity to Unity

The world is changing in rapid and unpredictable ways. Organisations that were once confident and assured of their own success, are now working hard to develop the flexibility to remain competitive and strategic in quickly changing circumstances. The diversity within organisations is also growing at an unparalleled rate. **Gone are the days of working with people who shared our same outlook, values, beliefs, and attitudes.** We now find ourselves working longer hours and under more pressure with people whom we understand less. Within any typical work group, it is now common to find people with significant differences in age, race, cultural background, nationality, and life experiences. Therefore it is critical that we learn to build connections and establish trust with people who have different life experiences, values and ideas.

As the diversity within organisations increases over the next twenty years, some organisations will create a significant business advantage by knowing how to foster relationships that generate confidence and rapport among diverse individuals and groups. Other organisations will fail, but not because they haven't tried. Much of the diversity work we see carried out in organisations today is focused almost entirely on people's differences. This approach often creates more barriers than it breaks down. **In *Creating the Energy of Connection*, we are moving the focus from what separates us to what connects us.** More than just a change in focus, it is a complete paradigm shift. Unity and connection are powerful experiences that bring us all closer to the essence of what it means to be human. Moreover, the field of quantum physics provides significant evidence that reality is not about separateness, but is in fact an intricate interplay of conscious intention and the interconnectedness of all things. According to the renowned quantum physicist David Bohm, "Unity and connectedness are key underlying principles of the universe." Recognizing and building on the notion that each one of us is *already connected* by virtue of a universal design is vital to making diversity work.

1

Quantum Physics (also called the New Science) is beginning to show us that the nature of the universe is constant change, and that who we are in any given moment is ever changing. Like all particles of nature, we too are never the same from one dynamic moment to the next. In fact, the stability of all nature depends on the abilities of its members to change. Margaret Wheatly, author of *Leadership and the New Science* writes,

> *"Strangely, the system maintains itself only if change is occurring somewhere in it all the time. New food sources, new neighbors, new talents appear. As conditions change, individuals experiment with new possibilities. If they fail to respond, the entire system suffers. An individual incapable of changing may disappear. Its demise will affect lives everywhere in the web."*

Dynamic change is a fact of life, and developing the skills and strategies to manage our selves and our relationships successfully is tantamount to our survival.

Quantum Physics also demonstrates that the blueprint for all of life is continuous relationship. We live in a relational world. Every tree, plant, animal, cell or organic compound needs to be in relationship to something else in order to survive and thrive. Nothing can exist alone. How we as individuals **choose** to be in relationship with each other is also essential. We make a choice as to what kind of relationships we want to create. Do we create healthy, nourishing relationships that elicit positive energy and opportunities for connections, or do we continue to fall back on reactive perceptions that constrict the flow of energy and possibility? Issues of diversity either push us forward into new arrangements for collaboration, or hold us back, because of our own discomfort with change and the unfamiliar.

The global workplace offers fertile ground to establish a new blueprint for change in human relationships. Everyday there are opportunities to not let the patterns of our past dictate our present behavior. By practising unity based relationship tools and strategies, rigid patterns of separation and control are unlocked allowing true human connection and authentic dialogue. **By consciously entering into diversity with the skills to truly exchange meaning with another human being unlike ourselves, we sow the seeds for the hope and growth of our planet.**

Much of the current training in diversity misses this opportunity for transformation. Focusing on people's differences places the spotlight on what is *not* common among us, and keeps the dialogue on a surface and intellectual level. This level doesn't provide individuals with a clear set of tools to create new patterns in relationships with others, because it does not provide individuals with the tools for creating new patterns within themselves.

In any dialogue on diversity, it is essential that we discuss and make known our differences—our different life experiences, viewpoints, values and ideas are essential parts of ourselves. Yet, how are we to develop authentic connections and create shared meaning while the emphasis is on what is separate about us? As with any beautiful object we might create, like a chair, we can admire the intricacies of the carving on the back, the shape of the legs, or the polish of the wood; but what keeps the whole thing together is the glue—which is invisible. Similarly, in moving from diversity to unity, we need a connector. **The invisible glue that connects the diversity among us is embedded in the tools and strategies of *Creating The Energy of Connection.***

In order to successfully *Create The Energy of Connection,* there are five skill areas that we need to acquire. Each of these skill areas are developed in more detail throughout the remaining chapters of the book:

- Perceiving the world differently

- Creating new patterns

- Assuming positive intent

- Offering ourselves differently

- We are the people we've been waiting for

This new set of skills and tools is based on the notion that the individual is the one who must continually find within them a new vision of the world. It is about awakening within ourselves the desire to go past what on the surface seems like a justifiable reason for shutting down or cutting someone off. When an encounter becomes difficult, it is easy to forget that we *do* have a choice to go beyond our conditioning and need for control. **But out of our fear, we often forego the opportunity to actually learn from another person who is different from ourselves.** Instead, we often defend our opinions in order to "be right," rather than listening to ideas and points of view that could take us to a deeper level of appreciation for someone else's experience. We then justify these defensive actions by telling ourselves the problem lies with the other person and their shortcomings. David Whyte, the poet and author of the *Heart Aroused,* brilliantly captures a moment when the possibility for a new connection and a new way to see a person is bypassed in favor of a desire for the familiar. He writes:

> *"Just the very moment we attempt to take a step in the right direction with a colleague, initiate a conversation, write a difficult memo, or take the first few steps in a new direction, we can suddenly feel that the chasm is insurmountable and the bridge we had hoped to cross is down."*

Diversity, by its very nature calls on us to create the connection when it isn't comfortable, when our best self isn't readily available—or worse—when we are already angry or mistrusting of a person or group because of past experiences. This is when the work of creating connections must be done with a new set of assumptions, skills and tools. In *Creating the Energy of Connection*, we focus not only on being open to others in order to access positive energy, but also on how each of us individually creates the opportunity that will enable us to be courageous, go beyond our fear, and create new possibilities in our relationships with others by being new in our relationship with ourselves.

Creating the Energy of Connection is about having an intentional relationship with ourselves—a relationship that creates the space for our interactions to be different because *we are different*. As individuals, we are the generators of the energy in any relationship. **Our choices, ideas, beliefs and needs enter into our encounters with others whether we are conscious of them or not.**

Creating the Energy of Connection is based on the notion that new possibilities emerge when we change *our perception of who we are*. Embedded in the five skill areas is the notion that perception is a powerful determinant of our experience. Nothing truly changes when we let our past behavior patterns determine our actions in the present. Diversity work means learning to look within ourselves to discover who we truly are, and what it is that drives our own perception. Understanding diversity while discovering patterns and dynamics *within us* creates a diversity journey—a journey that takes us beyond the common and the ordinary because in its fullest expression, it takes us beyond ourselves.

Each of the remaining chapters provides a number of simple, straightforward ideas and techniques that assist in the process of learning to successfully *Create the Energy of Connection*. These are called Key Tasks and follow each chapter's main ideas. By practising these Key Tasks, individuals will discover how to creatively manage their assumptions and biases while creating positive energy for themselves. With the ability to go past their biases, a wealth of positive energy is made available, and individuals can embrace diversity in their organisations and in their personal lives. In learning to *Create the Energy of Connection*, a good starting place is to begin looking at the power of perception, and the role it plays in our ability to create change within our selves, as well as connect with others in new ways.

2

Perceiving the World Differently

Perceptions create our world

What is perception? It is our interpretation of the world—but it is not the world itself. Perception is the lens through which we see our world. At any given moment, our perceptions are shaped by our beliefs, our emotions, and our past experiences. The assumptions and judgments that we make about others who are different from us are based on the messages and beliefs that we received as children, and continue to practise. **Our perceptions, then, are not truth. They are simply a culmination of our life lessons and experiences.** What a simple and marvelous realization. Understanding that perception is the lens through which we learn to see the world means that we can learn to operate this lens in ways that produce new perceptions and positive interactions with others. Recognizing the power of perception, we are more flexible, open-minded, and effective in working with others. By learning to harness the power of perception, we breakthrough to new thinking patterns, and our relationships have the possibility for new and more creative outcomes.

Throughout our childhood and adolescent years, we are continually bombarded with messages from parents, teachers, religious leaders and society in general about how to treat people. As we mature, we begin to filter out some of these messages and amend others. By the time we reach adulthood, we hold a view of the world that operates much like a photo-frame in front of us. It contains all our values, attitudes and beliefs, and informs us about appropriate ways to behave. We think we know how to operate in this world, feeling grown up and sure of our perceptions. The problem is our perceptions act as our truth. When someone comes along who is outside of our frame—someone different from us—we try to pull them into our frame and get them into focus. If we view them as more like us than different, then they can stay in our world and everything is fine. However, if we can't get them into focus, we leave them outside our world, *and view them as "wrong."* The following story, about two young men who received very different messages from their families about the value of personal property, illustrates how our childhood conditioning remains strong in adulthood and keeps us from interacting effectively with others whose life experience is different from our own.

Jim and Rich

Jim came from a very large family, having 11 brothers and sisters. In Jim's family, the emphasis was on sharing everything. None of the children in Jim's family had their own room, and some siblings shared the same bed. The first person up in the morning had the choice of the best clothes available, and who ever shouted the loudest was the one who was heard. The older siblings looked out for the younger ones. It was a family with a strong value of shared property. Jim grew up very comfortable in this world.

Conversely, Rich grew up an only child, and was taught consistently that what's yours is yours and you are responsible for your own things. He was taught not to borrow anything unless absolutely necessary, and, if so, he should take very good care of it and give it back on time. Also, when lending anything, Rich was taught to keep a record of it, and make sure he got it back on time. Rich's family placed a high value on individual property and personal space. Just like Jim, Rich grew up very comfortable in this world.

At eighteen, these two young men found themselves in college together sharing a house—including a kitchen. One morning, Rich put a yogurt in the fridge for later in the day. Jim came home hungry, looked in the fridge, and saw the yogurt. He thought, "I'm going to the store soon, I'll get some more yogurt then," and he ate the yogurt. Rich came home looking for his yogurt, and the following conversation begins:

Rich:	"Didn't I leave a yogurt in the fridge?"
Jim:	"Oh, yeah, I ate it, but I'm going to the store to get some more later today."
Rich:	"What? You ate my yogurt?"
Jim:	"Yeah, like I said, I'm going to the store shortly. Just give me a half an hour."
Rich:	"Just a minute—I really need to be clear about this. I have a yogurt, which *is mine*, and you come and take

	and eat *my* yogurt. Now am I right or have I missed something?"
Jim:	"Look, yogurts come in packs of eight. When I go to the store, I'll get whatever flavor you want, and you can have the whole thing."
Rich:	"No, you are completely missing the point, which is: You stole my yogurt."
Jim:	"We're talking about a yogurt here. I said I'd get you one as soon as I can. What's your problem anyway?"

The problem here is that Jim and Rich are each carrying a different value from their childhood about the ownership and sharing of personal property: Most important, they each measure the other against their own values, and then make the other person *wrong*. They both think they have the answer to the problem. Rich's stance is: "If you will only learn to respect my property, we'll get on just fine." Jim's stance is: "If you would be less selfish and learn to share more we could get on just fine."

As we see, they both think, *"You change. Then, you are in focus in my world and I'm happy. I don't have to change at all—because I am the one who is in the right on this."* **We do this all the time and call it diversity work—giving the other person information so they will change, and we will be more comfortable with them.**

It's not me who needs to change

Every day in the workplace, we see interactions between individuals and groups that follow the same course as Rich and Jim. People locked in conversations that are unproductive—even hostile—and driven by their assumptions and beliefs about how the world *should* be. These dialogues seldom create understanding about each other's differences, nor do they result in creative problem solving strategies. The reason is that most people do not recognize that their perceptions—their conditioning and beliefs—are the driving cause of their communication difficulties. Becoming aware of how our perceptions affect our behavior, we recognize that diversity work is learning to shift our expectations from how others need to change to looking at our own perceptions first.

As a result, we gain insight into how often our conditioning, more than the actual situation is the cause of our discomfort. **Effective diversity work in**

organisations means that individuals recognize *they* have the power to create new perceptions—perceptions that are based on inclusiveness and acceptance, allowing individuals to be different, but not wrong.

Does this mean then that we can never object to some-one else's behavior? Does it mean that we must let everyone off the hook, regardless? No. Clearly, organisations must have behavioral policies that establish clear boundaries for appropriate and inappropriate behavior in the workplace. And it is crucial that we continue to challenge racist, sexist and other derogatory behavior. Understanding perception in diversity work means that while we continue to challenge and confront issues of inequality and disrespect, we also pay attention to our own beliefs and values, and how they are impacting our decisions about the other person.

What if either Rich or Jim had been able to reflect on his reaction during their argument? What if either one of them had the awareness that it was their values and beliefs causing the conflict? From this reflection and awareness, their conversation could have shifted from accusations and blame to a discussion about their different upbringings, and how they each have very different ideas about sharing personal property. Even if only one of them had remained aware, it could have shifted the dynamics of the conversation in a way that positively impacted them both. This is the power of perception in diversity work. **It only takes one person to shift the energy towards understanding and connection, and any of us can choose to be that person, in any situation.** While this is not always easy, it is always possible.

In pursuing the unity within diversity, we learn to view our deeply held childhood and cultural beliefs as important parts of ourselves, but not as the totality of who we are. We can't change what has happened to us, nor can we remove our deep conditioning. We can, however, learn to bring our conditioned beliefs and expectations into conscious awareness, and recognize them for what they are—preconceived ideas about how we think the world should be. We may choose to continue holding some of these (or even all of these) as important perceptions of the world, but now it is a choice and we hold them less tightly. This process opens a space inside of us, and this space provides fertile ground for new awareness and new choices to arise. Now, we can consciously shift our perception towards kindness and openness, and become willing to go past our judgments, our attack thoughts, and our emotional dramas. This is how changing ourselves first opens the space for new possibilities to emerge in our relationships with others.

Staying aware of our conditioned attitudes and beliefs allows us to consciously choose perceptions that create possibility. **By being aware of our perceptions,**

and making a conscious choice to set aside our judgments, we become different. The possibility now exists for authentic dialogue with another person. We
can listen and learn about their different views of the world, even when these
views are in direct opposition to our own. We can find out the reasons why they
came to view the world so differently, and seek understanding rather than judgment. This involves the ability to listen at a new level. This ability is tied directly
to the previous work of shifting our perceptions and creating inner space.

Authentically connecting with different kinds of people generates the invisible
glue that holds our myriad of differences together. Depending on how our
upbringing and perceptions have constructed our world, we'll either accept or
reject certain people. Understanding the power of perception provides the natural
glue of connection that helps us go past our first impressions, and allows difficult
and challenging diversity situations to become opportunities for understanding.
More important, by shifting the focus to ourselves and consciously managing our
perceptions, we automatically align ourselves with a number of key quantum
principles underlying the nature of reality.

Science, reality and connectedness

As stated earlier, Quantum Physics is the study of matter or energy at the subatomic level. Quantum theory demonstrates that reality—at its most fundamental level—is not stationary, static or predictable. There is no cause and effect at
the subatomic level because the nature of reality is not a linear process. **In the
quantum world, matter, or what we think of as physical reality, is a complex
interplay of possibilities coming into existence.** Matter and energy are constantly switching between particles (matter) and waves (energy) and back again.
In the quantum realm, energy and matter exist not as predictable patterns, but as
information and pure potentiality. Moreover, whatever energy and matter is
manifested into being is a direct result of our observation. It is the act of measure-
ment or observation that causes a possibility to become actualized in the quantum realm. In other words, quantum physics demonstrates that we influence
what comes into existence by our participation in it. Describing some implica-
tions of quantum physics, author David Lewis writes: "He (David Bohm), like
Noble Laureate and renowned physicist Brian Josephson, saw that physics must
see the nature of subatomic reality in a new way. It is not simply that conscious
perspective affects the nature of the subatomic quanta, Bohm revealed, but that
the subatomic quanta is conscious, which means that everything is conscious,

even inanimate objects and seemingly empty space, the very definition, if one were possible, of mystical or spiritual reality."

Deepak Chopra, M.D., in his writings on the mind/body connection, provides helpful translations for the layperson on these technical aspects of quantum physics. In his book, *How to Know God*, he writes:

> *"The quantum realm is the fountainhead of pure potentiality, giving rise to the raw material of your body, your mind, and the physical universe. The quantum realm is the womb of creation, the invisible world where the visible is designed and assembled. In the quantum realm there are no fixed objects, only possibilities. The true nature of reality is the field of all possibilities where everything is interwoven and inseparably one. "*

In the quantum realm, an event is a particle and a wave simultaneously, and space and time are not fixed, but are interwoven and inseparable possibilities. A particle and a wave cannot be observed at the same time because they do not exist independently—nor do they act as themselves until they are observed. We must *choose* to see one or the other. **It is our intention that determines whether a particle or a wave comes into being by which one we choose to see.** In the quantum world, an observer is needed to create an event, and all events are virtual events until the moment they are observed. **We are direct participants in what we experience.**

By understanding this level of reality, we begin to appreciate the power of bringing new patterns into our relationships by consciously directing our perceptions and our intentions. Our perceptions and our reactions *are* our reality and make up our world. Real power lies in our ability to choose. We can decide what we perceive, how we want to react, and what we want to bring into reality through our conscious participation in it. In learning to *Create the Energy of Connection*, we are changing our habitual reactions and consciously shifting our perceptions. These changes create a new energy and give us information, leading us to new ways of relating. In *Creating the Energy of Connection,* we recognize that no matter how much we disagree with someone or are upset about something they have done, it is our mental and emotional reactions that form the basis of our reality, a reality that comes from our perception. *Creating the Energy of Connection* is about cleaning up our instrument of perception, and viewing our thoughts and feelings as information about ourselves—our beliefs, values, and assumptions—and not as accurate pictures of reality. Noticing, and consciously managing our mental and emotional reactions, opens space for creating understanding of another person's life experiences, and unlocks our awareness of the unity that is already there. **Wholeness and unity are the foundations of reality at its most basic level.** It is only at the individual level that we create the notion of separateness.

Understanding and incorporating these quantum principles into our relationships is part of the new work in diversity. In this paradigm, relationships become a mirror—a way for us to see ourselves reflected in the situations that present themselves. We manage relationships from the perspective of what *our* reactions, feelings and beliefs say about *us* before considering what the other person's behavior says about them. We realize we are instrumental in what happens to us, and relationships are an *outcome* of our choices and a reflection of our inner states, and not things that exist outside of us and can be molded like clay. Our reactions provide us with vital information because they are a direct feedback loop presenting us with specific data on the kinds of seeds we are sowing. Our relationships show up as we set them up. We can either create opportunities for open-mindedness, understanding and connection, or we can blame the other person, and remain unaware of how our unchecked perceptions and assumptions contribute to the dynamics we find ourselves enmeshed in. The following story illustrates the power of perception and choice as the keys to creating unity out of diversity.

Miranda and Cindy

Miranda and Cindy were attorneys working for a legal aid organisation. Miranda, an African American woman was Cindy's manager. Cindy, a Caucasian woman, didn't like Miranda's management style, and because she had been with the agency longer, Cindy also felt she should be given more freedom.

Over time, Cindy became resentful of Miranda's management style, feeling that Miranda "micro-managed" her. As the manager, Miranda felt that Cindy wasn't doing all she could to inform her and keep her abreast of her projects. Their differences in style escalated and created significant strain and tension on the team. While their differences in style could have happened between any manager and employee regardless of color or background, Miranda and Cindy also recognized that their different racial orientations contributed significantly to their inability to find common ground. After one particularly tense team meeting, the team decided to call in a diversity expert to help. They contacted us.

Our main strategy was to work with Miranda and Cindy in a "dialogue session"—a guided process for helping individuals listen past their current beliefs, expectations and reactions. As the dialogue session began, Miranda described her "amazement" about Cindy's "cavalier" attitude about her assignments, and disrespecting her opportunity to demonstrate her competence in every aspect of her job—including turning in her billing time records, and weekly reports. Cindy's response was typical. She was "baffled" by how Miranda was so "short-sighted," paying attention to aspects of the job Cindy felt had nothing to do with her competence as an attorney. In addition, Cindy was particularly upset that Miranda never congratulated her on her recently published article, one that had earned accolades from her peers.

As the dialogue continued, we asked Miranda and Cindy to repeat what they each heard the other saying. **As is typical in this first level of dialogue, what each of them heard the other saying was that basically the other person was wrong.** Miranda heard Cindy say she shouldn't be so nit-picky. Cindy heard Miranda telling her that her job priorities were wrong. At this level of perception, neither was willing to budge.

At the next level of the dialogue, they were assisted in listening beyond their habitual responses and to look at their own reactions. Through this process, Miranda and Cindy began to hear and understand each other at a new level.

As the two women began to talk more honestly about their true feelings, what began to emerge was recognition that there *were things* about the other that each could truly understand and respect. Cindy told Miranda how it hurt her that Miranda never mentioned or gave her recognition for the article she published. Miranda began to talk about her own childhood and how she was raised to "not expect any pats on the back," and so she didn't think to give them to others. Miranda went on to say that, as a black woman in her mid-50's, she had been raised to believe that "if you wait for somebody to give you credit, you will never go anywhere." Miranda considered herself successful because she *didn't need* recognition from others. Cindy was surprised and taken aback. **It had never occurred to her that Miranda's behavior was driven by a completely different set of life experiences and messages.**

Cindy began to describe the messages that she received as a child about success. Cindy said she was one of three daughters from a white, middle-class, "emotionally open and nurturing family." Cindy and her sisters always received great recognition from both parents, but particularly from their father, who was also an attorney. Cindy learned to expect recognition for all of her accomplishments especially from the person in authority. At this point, Miranda began to understand and appreciate how Cindy had received a different set of messages about success, and therefore had a different set of expectations in the workplace.

Through a continued dialogue, the two women began to see each other for who they really were and discovered things in each other that they could understand, learn from, and respect. This greatly improved their working relationship and their ability to communicate and solve problems effectively. Their professional relationship grew into a special friendship.

One year later, when Miranda was diagnosed with breast cancer, she asked Cindy to be her main support person through the treatment process. For the next fifteen months, Cindy accompanied Miranda to all her appointments, and provided ongoing help, nurturing and support. At Miranda's funeral, Cindy spoke. She talked of her experience with Miranda, a person she thought she would never understand or like. She said that learning to listen to someone's different background and upbringing brought her the gift of Miranda's friendship. She said she would never judge anyone again, and work to understand people's differences.

Differences will always tempt us toward the illusion of separateness. Miranda and Cindy were both caught in perceptions driven by their childhood conditioning and their different life experiences. The resolution of their conflict did not come from each of them stating and then re-stating their current beliefs and perceptions of the other. Resolution came from being able to listen beyond their current beliefs and perceptions. This is how diversity and unity work together. Whenever we deal with a diverse person who makes us uncomfortable, we will be tempted to believe that the person is causing our discomfort, which isn't the case. **The reality is that our discomfort comes from our interpretation of what the person is saying or doing.** When we see our own conditioning, and the biases and perception it creates, we free up inner space to learn about the other person and how they see the world. This process brings about the quantum leap.

Creating the Energy of Connection is about recognizing who we really are. Our different life experiences are very real, and they form a significant portion of our identity, our expectations of the world, and our reactions, but they are not the essence of who we are. **Our essence is simply pure potentiality inherent in the energy and intelligence of the universe.** The more identified we are with our differences and our personal stories, the less easy it is to create space within, and appreciate other people's perspectives as valid. If we are going to use the tools and techniques for creating new connections successfully, we need to be aware of the power that perception carries—especially about things that we are extremely attached to. In this regard, we must also learn to be smart about our egos, and understand how they influence our perceptions, and set us up to repeat ineffective behavioral patterns.

Perception and the ego

The term ego is used in many ways. Our use of the term describes that part of us that desires to be separate, and strongly resists when we start moving to new levels of growth and change. In her book, *Comfortable With Uncertainty*, the Buddhist nun, Pema Chodron, describes the ego in a way that is very similar to our use of the term. She writes:

> *"Resistance is the fundamental operating mechanism of the ego. Traditionally, it is said that the cause of suffering is clinging to our own narrow point of view, which is to say that we are addicted to ME. We resist the truth that actually, we all change and flow like the weather, and that we all have the same energy as all living things. When we resist this idea, we dig in our heels. We make ourselves really solid. Resisting is what's called the ego."*

We are using the term ego to describe that part of ourselves that generates—and then clings to—a false belief that each of us is a separate identity and completely independent of each other. The ego believes in its own power alone, and wants to be in charge of its own destiny. The ego *does not want to know or sense* the unifying field that connects us all because then it would be faced with the reality that it is not in charge and running the show.

At the same time, our egos are very necessary to us. We need them to function in the world to get our basic needs met. It's useful to think of the ego as a huge pet dog—an amiable, but obedient companion. Yet, imagine that this dog were unruly, jumping up on people and all over the furniture. Our dog would be a nuisance and no one would want us to visit with it. So it is with our ego. **The ego needs to be our friend—but an obedient one. It should serve us, not drive us.**

It is helpful to be aware that the ego is always concerned with establishing a hierarchy of worth. In the ego's eyes someone *always* needs to be a "more than" and someone else a "less than." This ensures that we remain separate from other people, and not inclined to see what we have in common and connect with them at a new level. The ego wants us to believe that this hierarchy of worth is real—thus distorting our perceptions towards its singular purpose of remaining in control. Separation and control are the ego's life force. The ego does not like it when we decide to change *ourselves*, instead of focusing on another person's faults and shortcomings. It suits the ego to keep us focused on someone else because the ego can keep us trapped in the illusion that by changing the other person (which is in fact impossible), we never have to challenge the direct source of our pain and confusion—our own perceptions and conditioned beliefs. Instead, the ego wants us to invest in the false belief that we must control others or else they will control us. It is important to remember that by taking responsibility for our perceptions and working to create more inner space, the ego will not be happy. By design, the ego will feel threatened by all the possible new solutions, connections and outcomes previously unknown to you. Looking to change others, rather than ourselves, the ego keeps our perception trapped in the illusion that if we can get someone else to change then we will be happy. **The ego's only concept of love and connection involves expectations, possessiveness, sacrifice, measurements and proofs.**

After operating from ego for so long, we need to remember that in *Creating the Energy of Connection,* we are using tools and strategies that are completely outside the ego's main purpose of being in control. These ideas, and the Key Tasks we recommend, are outside the ego's comfort zone because they have nothing to do with getting others to change or being smarter about getting what we want. Practising the Key Tasks is about changing ourselves, and trusting that in doing so, everything else will change in its own right way. Your ego will hate this.

In *Creating the Energy of Connection,* we are learning to operate outside the ego's world of control, and opening up to the parts of ourselves that are aligned with the unified field of all possibilities. And while this may be challenging, it doesn't have to be complicated. By practising even *one* of the Key Tasks, from *any of the chapters,* in any order, powerful changes can result. It can open the potential for new relationship patterns to emerge; patterns that are outside of the ego's fixed world of predictability and control. Practising any Key Task, in any situation, is a powerful first step towards experiencing new dynamics and outcomes in our relationships.

Your ego, however, is likely to be quite strong—you have had many years of building it up. So, throughout this book, we will give you warning bells by predicting some of the typical thoughts the ego will likely present in its attempts to stop you from putting these ideas into practice. The ego knows that once you shift your perceptions towards understanding, possibility, and the inherent unity of all things, it is completely doomed!

Iyanla Vanzant in her book, *One Day My Soul Just Opened Up,* writes a warning to the ego that captures its essence very well:

EGO..........

That part of us that continues to worry

Live in doubt

Is afraid

Judges other people

Is afraid to trust

Needs proof

Believes only when it is convenient

Fails to follow up

Refuses to practice what it preaches

Needs to be rescued

Wants to be a victim

Beats up on self

Needs to be right all of the time

And continues to hold on to what does not work

You are now put on notice that....

YOUR DAYS ARE NUMBERED

When we work to establish the Energy of Connection within ourselves, the ego *will* rear its ugly head. Some beliefs that the ego will use to keep us locked into a repetitive pattern of separation, self-righteousness, control and even attack are described below. We call these ego beliefs the "Let Go's" because they are common ego beliefs that we need to let go of in order to be able to create new patterns. In each of following chapters there will also be a list of Ego Beliefs to Let Go—related to that chapter's topic.

Ego Beliefs—Let Go's

"If something irritates us about another person, it is surely our job to tell them since they are the ones who need to change."

The funny thing about change is that we can only change ourselves. We can never *make* anyone change. We might put pressure on them to behave differently, but this doesn't guarantee they would change. Of course, when people are behaving inappropriately at work, we must challenge their behavior and take whatever steps are necessary to hold them accountable. And yet, how we go about doing this and the attitude we carry in the process is also our responsibility and will affect the outcome. **So whether we are challenging someone's behavior, or working to let go and see the situation differently, we have to take responsibility for our perceptions and our reactions. The bottom line is always that we can only change ourselves.**

"It is impossible to love everyone so this is all ridiculous"

The reason why we might want to let this belief go is that the ego uses it to keep us from reaching out to anyone—especially someone who causes us discomfort. So for now, let go of the idea that we have to love everyone, and just be willing to consider that if we don't like someone, it has more to do with us than it does with them. **It is true that we are not going to love everyone, but we can shift our perception to see what is positive in someone—even someone whose differences make us uncomfortable.** This is a small step in overcoming our ego's programming, and it often helps overcome our resistance to developing a relationship with someone.

"Not everything is a matter of opinion—some things are right and some things are wrong"

Yes it is certainly true that some things are right and some things are wrong as defined by parameters we need to live within—human rights, land, state laws, organisational rules, and departmental codes of conduct. These will be explicit and people need to know they will be held accountable to them. **However, many** things are not a matter of right or wrong, but are opinions and perceptions about what is right and wrong.

Remember the yogurt story? Jim and Rich each thought they were right. Jim felt that Rich was wrong to steal his property. Rich felt that people living in the same house share whatever food is there. Both of them were right and both of them were wrong *depending on whose lens you were looking through.* Pay attention to your expectations in relationships. Do you expect others to believe the same things as you? Are you uncomfortable with differences you don't know much about? **Believing that our ideas, values, and experiences are "the right ones" is a game the ego plays to keep us separate from others and feeling in control.**

Following are "Key Tasks" that you can start doing now to challenge your perceptions and begin to act differently.

KEY TASKS

Be willing to move out of denial

The starting point in diversity work is to accept that *each one of us* has work to do. The issue of diversity has been with us for so long that we tend to live in a complacent bubble of denial. We might admit that years ago we stereotyped people, but now we believe are "equality enlightened," and that we no longer judge people based on biases and stereotypes. In truth, we do it all the time. We need to get smart about when we do it. **We are all carrying around a huge bag of biases and judgments about other people.** And of course, they spill out all of the time. Those around us can see that we are burdened by the weight of them. We need to recognize when we are stereotyping, judging and showing our biases towards others. We need to take hold of the bag, open it voluntarily, have a good look around in there, and own what needs to be worked on.

Understand that by changing yourself you are changing what can happen next

Try the following experiment. Spend some time reflecting on the individuals at work that you exclude (yes—we all do this). Begin to identify the messages you tell yourself about this person. Write these thoughts down. Ask yourself what messages and beliefs you carry from your childhood that influence your current attitudes towards this person. Do you see any connections? Now, set these messages aside and intentionally notice something positive about the person. This may feel uncomfortable at first. You might even feel like you are being "dishonest" or not being "true to yourself." But, which is truer about a person—their good points or their bad points? Neither, as everyone has both positive and negative characteristics. **What we need to focus on instead is the truth about reality—that what we pay attention to is what comes into being.** By practising this technique, we simply allow the positive to show up. You might also find that the person seems sincerely more likable now just because you became different yourself.

Own the world you are in—and allow others to be in their world too

As we have seen, sometimes our perceptions are driven by the ego, and sometimes our perceptions are aligned with the truth that reality is simply a world of possibilities that we participate in creating. Owning our world means noticing what perceptual field we are operating from, and recognizing that we always have a choice. **Without judging ourselves, we accept responsibility for the world we see, and understand that our world is not the world.** Owning our perceptions, and knowing we are responsible for how we see the world, we recognize that others are also responsible for how they see their world. There is no right and wrong in these worlds—only differences. And yet, when people have very different ideas and values, the ego feels justified in seeing them as less than us, and believing they are wrong. In owning our world, we stay aware of our thinking—our judgments and biases—so we don't unconsciously project our attitudes on to other people and make them wrong. We recognize that people are never less than us, and they are not "wrong"—it is just that the aperture of their lens is set very differently from our own.

It is easy to get caught up in society's labels of who is a "more than" and who is a "less than," and forget that the ego and its dynamics operate the same way in every person no matter what their racial, socio-economic, or cultural differences. We were reminded of this recently while working in an inner-city community program. Two Native American women, each from a different regional tribe, refused to have lunch in the same room together because of their beliefs about the other.

See everything as interwoven and inseparably one

Quantum physics demonstrates that at its most fundamental level, reality is about unity, connectedness and the principle of co-creation. Even if we understand this at an intellectual level, it is still difficult to maintain this awareness when faced with someone who is different and around whom we feel uncomfortable. Our ego leads us to see them "out there," and we make judgments accordingly. However, by consciously shifting our focus to the wider more truthful perspective that we are all connected and every situation is just a reflection of our own perceptual field, we become the mirror. The situation reflects back to us our own expectations, beliefs and needs, and we begin to see the situation from the perspective of what we can learn about ourselves. When we are honest with ourselves, and we really look inside and see what's there, it frees us, and we can even wind up feeling gratitude for the awful situation that presented itself. **When we are willing to see everything as interwoven and inseparably one, our relationships become the mirrors that reflect our perceptions back to us so that we can make a choice, and act in new ways.** In this choice, we can also decide to offer ourselves differently. By consciously aligning our intention and our perceptions with these underlying principles of unity and connectedness, we become the means for transforming conflicts and difficulties into opportunities for understanding and appreciation.

3

Creating New Patterns

To successfully change our behavior over the long term is often a difficult and challenging process. Often, we set out to break a habit or begin acting in a new way, only to wind up back where we started—feeling frustrated and defeated. The latest research on the brain helps us to understand how to make our efforts to change our behavior more successful by re-patterning our brains—especially our "emotional brain."

Recent research on the brain demonstrates that for every experience we have, the brain creates a set of corresponding neurological pathways for that experience. **The more we engage in certain behaviors or activities, the more the corresponding neurological pathways in the brain are reinforced.** The brain then begins to favor these well-traveled neurological connections over other less traveled pathways. It's as if these well-traveled pathways become "hardwired" into the brain, and it takes very little conscious intention to direct our behavior in these activities. For example, have you ever driven somewhere, and when you arrived, realized that you have no memory of the actual route you took? This is because when we travel a route many times, the brain's neural connections are so accustomed to the set of actions that our conscious minds are free to do other things while we are driving: plan a vacation, rehearse an upcoming conversation or daydream. If we suddenly decide to take a new route, we would have to exert more conscious effort, as the neurological connections for this route would not yet be established. **To make a change in a behavior that is deeply ingrained in the neurological networks of our brain takes a very conscious intention.** In addition, the cultural, religious, and family messages that we have internalized become entrenched in our neural pathways, also causing our thinking patterns to become conditioned and automatic. As a result of these established pathways in the brain, we may find it extremely uncomfortable to challenge our assumptions about the world—even in the face of strong evidence that it would be advantageous to do so. Consider the story of Joseph, a middle manager in a Fortune 500 company.

Joseph

Joseph came to us for a series of diversity coaching sessions. Although technically very good at his job and always on time, Joseph's teammates complained that he was overly aggressive, even hostile, and that he did not work co-operatively. In fact, his direct reports had ceased wanting to work with him.

Our conversations with Joseph taught us many things. His family and cultural background led him to believe that he must "win at all costs," and that it was up to him to make things happen. Joseph believed that if he didn't "compete to be the best" he wasn't living up to the ideals of his father, or any of the men in his family.

We began a coaching process with Joseph that would enable him to act in new ways and develop his skills as an effective team leader. Unfortunately, Joseph did not see this opportunity for growth. He continued to believe the message his family and culture had taught him. He also thought the company's focus on "all this time consuming team stuff" was just another trend that would get in the way of bottom line efficiency.

Joseph left the company with his strong belief in the power of competitiveness and aggression intact. Nothing could change his belief. All the feedback from his team, his boss and his colleagues did nothing to convince Joseph that he was a big part of the problem. Joseph could only see that the *company's approach was wrong,* and that *he was right.*

Still, you might ask, didn't Joseph have a right to dislike the style of the company he worked in and therefore leave it for a job he would be more comfortable with? Absolutely. However, Joseph did not *choose* to leave based on this aware-ness. **Joseph left unaware of how his beliefs impeded his ability to listen and understand** his colleagues' experiences and feedback. Joseph believes his percep-tion of the company is "truth," and thus, he will continue to perpetuate his belief that his independence and aggressiveness are never a part of the problem. Fur-ther, these conditioned attitudes and beliefs will prevent him from solving rela-tionship problems with others.

Joseph's behavior and thinking processes were deeply ingrained in well-estab-lished neural pathways. For him to go against long-standing and deeply pro-grammed messages would have created a strong sense of unfamiliarity and discomfort. This would be difficult for any of us. When we begin to challenge our assumptions and deeply held beliefs about the world, our perceptions are impacted by the brain's preference for already established thinking and behavioral pathways. In addition, the brain has evolved sophisticated mechanisms for survival that continue to influence our behavior and impede our ability to easily embrace the unknown.

The evolution of the brain

Over the past several hundred million years, our brains have evolved into three distinct regions—the reptilian brain (the lower brain), the limbic brain (the middle region), and the neo-cortex (the frontal lobe area). Each one of these three brains still operates and strongly influences our perceptions, our experiences, and our behavior.

The reptilian—or oldest brain—is directly tied to our nervous system, and directs our behavior by instinct. Before we could communicate with pictures or with sophisticated language, the reptilian brain kept us alive. If we saw a bear, we did not have the neurological capacity to think, "*Oh there's a bear.*" All we had was our reptilian brain signaling our muscles and nervous system to decide between two classic responses: fight or flight. **The fight or flight response is still our brain's primary reaction when we are faced with danger or a threat—whether the threat is real or imagined.** We instinctively carry this fight or flight response into our relationships with others.

The limbic—or middle brain—is more evolved than the reptilian brain, but operates without sophisticated language. In our evolution as a species, the limbic brain developed during our early communal stages arising from our need to communicate with groups that were unfamiliar. The key to the development of these communal societies was the ability to sense a good personal association from a bad one. Evolutionarily, the limbic region stored the recording of positive and negative feelings, and served to guide us into relationships with those outside our group who gave us a positive feeling or impression. To this day, the limbic brain records all of our emotional experiences and creates a set of hard-wired emotional patterns that can be triggered in similar circumstances. Limbic-based communication was based on pictures, drawings, and rituals.

The neo-cortex—the more recently developed brain—is the seat of all our higher cognitive functions. In fact, the functions of the neo-cortex are what we think of as intelligence itself. The neo-cortex gives us the capability to reason, structure time, abstract ideas, imagine, create, and reflect on the consequences of our actions. The neo-cortex is the part of our brain that is capable of observing and evaluating whether our own behavior is in line with our intentions and our core values. The neo-cortex gives us the ability to see who we want to be in the future, and make the connection between positive changes in our behavior and experiencing different outcomes. However, this process can be interrupted when either the reptilian or limbic regions of the brain are triggered by threats—real or imagined. All of our good intentions and our reflective capabilities can be overtaken by these more primal systems, and can cause us to act in ways that are not in our own best interests. Some brain researchers call this process "emotional hijacking." The reptilian and limbic regions of the brain are geared toward survival, and eliminating or reducing the source of the threat. Joseph's unwillingness to even consider his colleagues' feedback is indicative of behavior that is tied closely to the brain's defense systems.

In our current evolution, every one of us is a combination of all three brains. **Our past is deeply ingrained in the fabric of our cellular structures.** A critical step in creating behavior patterns more helpful to diversity is to understand how different parts of our brain create different kinds of perceptions. When we are threatened, defensive, or afraid, our emotions will be disturbed, and our perceptions will also disturbed and often laced with blame, accusations, judgments and a desire to find fault. **Awareness of our emotions and thoughts is a key to understanding what is driving our perceptual field.** Are our survival mechanisms driving our perceptions? If so, we need to shift our perceptual field so that our lens can generate openness, consideration, thoughtfulness and compassion. When we feel tense and constricted—even if we feel absolutely certain that we are right—it is a strong clue that our primordial defense systems are in control and need to be settled down. These processes happen quickly and require that we constantly check in with ourselves to see what our reactions are to people and their differences. Many of the Key Tasks in this book can help us to do this.

Our world is made up of our conditioned attitudes and beliefs

We could make a long list of all the differences in the world, and all the various ways we might react to these differences. Some of our reactions would be to differences that are immediately obvious—things like gender, skin color, height, weight, body language, accent, tattoos, and piercings. Other reactions would be to differences we discover only when someone tells us about them—differences such as educational background, marital status, sexual orientation, or political persuasion. In either case, the brain sends us strong signals, and instantaneously, any one of these differences could cause us to feel extremely uncomfortable.

For example, we might really like a person's accent, and that would be a difference we feel comfortable with. We might even feel warm towards this person and drawn to knowing more about them. On the other hand, long hair on a man might make us uncomfortable, causing us to act cold or distant towards him. In addition, if we feel very strongly about a particular aspect of difference—tattoos or piercings for example—then we might quickly decide against the person, and close ourselves off. The brain signals these positive and negative reactions immediately—and via mechanisms that involve very little conscious thought. In *Creating the Energy of Connection*, it is critical to begin uncovering the thoughts and feelings that exist just below the surface of our conscious awareness. A simple yet powerful strategy for bringing our thought processes more into our conscious awareness is to create an "interesting box." For example, we might hear ourselves saying, "I can't stand people who are covered with tattoos and piercings." Noticing the thought, we can say to ourselves "that's interesting" and put it in the box. Doing this helps us detach from the emotional energy of the thought, and opens a space for us to ask ourselves *why* we feel so strongly about this particular difference.

Whenever we have an impulse to pull away, and not want to move toward someone who looks different, we are in a position to learn about ourselves. This impulse to pull away is a signal to pay attention to our thoughts. Once we notice our thoughts, we can learn to recognize our deeply patterned beliefs and attitudes. We then gain new information about ourselves, and create opportunities for new choices in our behavior. And yet, we often don't view our reactions as information about ourselves. Instead, we let the reptilian brain take over, and we judge the person with the difference as the problem.

Whenever we are extremely uncomfortable with someone's differences, it can trigger emotionally charged patterns *in us*. When *our* strong beliefs are hooked, the reptilian brain rushes in to ensure our survival by reducing any threats—real or imaginary. **The brain quickly takes us from noticing a difference, to interpreting it as a threat, and determining we must win (be right).** Our perceptual field begins to constrict, and the person with the difference *becomes the problem*. In that moment, we have completely lost any opportunity to learn about ourselves. Instead, our world becomes a potential battlefield. This is the process of every human being on the planet. How can we ever live together harmoniously when we unconsciously let our reptilian brains drive our perceptions? Unless we learn to recognize our uncomfortable feelings, tune into our inner experience, and connect the dots of our own reactions, we are destined to live in a global community of irresolvable conflicts. This is doing our own diversity work—and as we say throughout this book—there is no other work to do. Every day our hard-wired beliefs and unmanaged habitual thoughts create conflicts and misunderstandings in the workplace. Consider the situation of Silla, a young Asian woman working in a large company as a manager of Information Technology.

Silla and Linda

Silla's parents emigrated to America from China, and Silla was born and raised in the United States. Silla grew up very comfortable with the American lifestyle. However, her parents kept a very traditional Chinese household, and Silla received strong messages about traditional Chinese culture. At home, Silla was taught to treat her parents, her parents' friends, and her older relatives with a level of respect that is not the norm in the American culture. As a result, Silla sometimes found it difficult to assert herself and be direct with people in her organisation who were her "superiors."

During her annual performance review, Silla's boss, Linda, mentioned to Silla that she needed to become "more assertive." Silla listened to the feedback and knew that Linda's feedback was accurate—this was not a new awareness for her. Silla also knew that her lack of assertiveness was directly related to her cultural upbringing, something she had been working on for a while. Silla decided to take a risk. She told Linda she agreed with the feedback, and began to share with Linda some of the conflict she found herself in as the result of being raised in two different cultures. Silla hoped that sharing this information with Linda, would allow them to come up with strategies to help Silla be more effective in her challenging managerial role. Through the lens of her own past conditioning Linda said, "It must be really weird to have parents that don't think like the rest of the world. I can't imagine that. Thank goodness, my parents taught me to stand up to anyone and everyone who should be challenged." Silla went quiet. She knew that Linda didn't mean to be offensive—that she was blinded by her own past conditioning—but it hurt nevertheless. Silla realized that her boss didn't really see her for who she was—a motivated employee with a specific kind of problem—a problem that Linda had never experienced. Further, because Linda had not learned to notice her reaction, her thoughts and feelings, she wasn't able to listen past her own experience and understand Silla's problem. Through her constricted lens, Linda saw Silla as unfortunate for receiving messages from parents who were "wrong." Linda did not see Silla's willingness to share how her upbringing was creating difficulty on the job as an opportunity. Instead, Linda saw it as confirmation or evidence that Silla was odd or a "less than." **All Linda needed to do was notice that her first thought was a judgment, and put it in her "interesting box." This would have created an internal space for her to make a different choice.** She could have asked a question or simply let Silla continue talking. Either way, Linda would have opened the possibility for a new perception of Silla—one in which Silla is a person with a story to tell. A story that is unique and interesting in its own right. Listening past her judgment, Linda could have challenged the belief that her upbringing was the "right" one. If she had noticed her judgment and put it in her interesting box, Linda might have learned something she didn't know before, and recognized the common human emotions that Silla was feeling.

With the world becoming smaller every day, and with our work processes connecting us more easily around the globe, we continue to come in contact with differences that cause strong reactions. Doing diversity work isn't going to be easy. We all carry strong messages and experiences from our childhood that spill over into our workplace relationships. In dealing with our particular individual messages, we also need to be aware of beliefs that many of us may have about groups of people. Here are some examples of hard-wired beliefs about groups of people that create judgments, blame, conflicts, and misunderstandings on the job:

• Women will quit their job to have children, so they shouldn't be taken as seriously as men.

• People of color are not as hard working as Caucasians.

• People who speak with an accent give the company a bad name.

• Black people are angry.

• White men can't be trusted.

• People who are late are disorganized and disrespectful.

• Her size will give the wrong impression to clients.

• Young people have no work ethic.

• Homosexuals are not normal.

- People who don't work as hard as I do are lazy.

- All Muslims are trained to hate.

- Well-dressed people are trustworthy.

- His father is a great employee therefore he will be too.

- People who go to church on Sunday are moral and good.

- Black boys standing in a group are gang members.

- The workplace is not for getting to know people.

- People who take time to think before they speak are slow.

This list could go on forever. We all carry a huge bag full of these messages, and they get in the way of our ability to connect and bring out the best in each other. **There will always be reasons to keep our limited perceptions and never move into the energy of connection.** Most of these reasons will be tied closely to our hard-wired patterns. Without conscious awareness and intention on our part, our perceptions will be locked into a narrow focus of right and wrong, good and bad, and more than/less than while the potential for a relationship of learning and growth will not happen. **From a work standpoint, the inability to change our perceptions prevents personal and professional growth, which undermines business growth.** Critical to our diversity work is the ability to recognize where our perceptions are coming from, and consciously choose to see each other's humanity, and recognize the truth of our connectedness.

So what ego beliefs do we need to let go of in order to create new patterns?

Ego Beliefs—Let Go's

"If I feel something very strongly then it must be true"

Our instincts are critically important and have served us well over the course of our evolution. However, the next stage of our evolution is a tricky one. **To become a peaceful, viable, global community, we have to learn to use our instincts to establish connectedness, not separation.** The "fight or flight" response will always remain a primary one within us, and it is an excellent response when there is the possibility of real danger. Hearing a loud, strange noise in the middle of the night awakens our instincts appropriately. Without having to think, we are naturally charged with adrenalin and energy as our bodies prepare—in an instant—to do whatever is necessary to survive. So we must learn to identify those life situations where this kind of response is helpful—in danger and crises situations. In our personal and professional relationships, however, the "fight or flight" response is not helpful, except, of course, when we encounter the threat of physical, verbal or emotional abuse. Otherwise it is never a good instinct to follow.

When we are charged with strong, driven, opinionated energy in our thoughts—and we are not managing it—we will almost always engage in some form of attack or withdrawal in our behavior towards others. The energy driving our behavior is our survival instinct. Once we are sure that we are *right,"* and we feel compelled to convince someone at all costs, the fight or flight response is engaged. When this happens, our perception locates the *evidence* that the other person *should be different* and show us how they *deserve* to be corrected. There-fore, we feel justified in either attacking them with shaming aggressive remarks, or, we employ the flight response and leave them out of the loop, forget to call them back, or neatly amputate them from our lives without ever saying a word. **In either case, we have lost the opportunity to learn about the inner work-ings of our own perceptual lens, and the ability to *Create the Energy Of Con-nection* when a conflict or difficulty arises.**

"Some people deserve to be punished and it's my job to do it"

Obviously, anyone who has broken a law, broken a formal agreement, or acted outside of a policy must pay the consequences for their behavior. Yet, we see many people who carry the belief that they are the watchdogs for other people's behavior. When someone's behavior does not conform to their idea of what is right and appropriate, they see it as their job to give the person "feed-back"—often a code word for telling someone they should *do it my way*. Interest-ingly, people with this belief often use pouting, resentment and scorn to communicate their disapproval thereby hiding from themselves that they actually engage is this behavior. **We need to give up the belief that we are the watch-dogs for other people's personal preferences.**

"You can't expect me to ditch attitudes and values I've had for years"

We are not asking you to give up attitudes and values that you have had for years. We are asking you to remember that, for most of us, our childhood conditioning, and the messages we received from our parents and communities about diverse people, were usually emotionally loaded. Every memory has an emotional element and our emotional experiences are set into the brain's neurological patterns with more intensity and more distinctive pathways than those that lack an emotional element. **Most important to remember is that we always have a choice in terms of how to react to someone.**

"Even if I wanted to change—it's too hard at my age"

Re-patterning our reactions does take time because it involves an ongoing practice of trial and error. Yet eventually, the new re-patterned pathways become familiar and new habits set in. **Our ability to change is tied to our present beliefs about ourselves—beliefs about who we think we are.** Am I the kind of person that can live with repeated attempts and a number of failures? How do I handle things not going right the first time, the second time, the ninth time? What do I do when an old pattern sucks me in just when I thought it was conquered? These beliefs reflect our *willingness to* change, not our *ability to* change. **The commitment to change can be made in one second—with one thought.** People who say they can't change are usually talking about their experience with the re-patterning process. They have confused the practice of trial and error with a belief about their own capability. A very big change does take time, but with a little willingness, we can renew our commitment to the practice, and eventually we get it right enough times that our brains begin working in our favor. Following are some Key Tasks to assist us in the change process.

KEY TASKS

Pay attention to your emotions

Our thoughts and feelings are closely tied together. Sometimes, it is difficult to actually hear what we are saying to ourselves because our thoughts are buried under strong emotions, like fear, anger, or severe disappointment. When we are not sure how our thoughts are contributing to our current perceptions, it is useful to tune into our feelings, by paying close attention to the way the body is responding. The body does not lie—it is an absolute barometer of our true reactions. Noticing our breathing, our heart rate, our tone of voice and the level of tension in our muscles provides direct clues to our feeling state and associated thoughts. **The more we can decode our reactions by uncovering our thoughts and feelings, the more information we gain about ourselves.** By opening up and consciously examining our views of the world, we can decide how well our conditioned perceptions serve us—or don't serve us—in making connections with others who are very different from ourselves.

Identify your own biases

Spend some time reflecting on the individuals at work that you exclude (yes—we all do this). Identify some messages and beliefs that you have about these people. What do you notice? Are your current attitudes towards this person being driven by messages from your upbringing? Is it actually *your beliefs* that are creating a disconnection? Are these differences simply a challenge to *your own* emotionally hard-wired beliefs? Consider Diane who came from a home where messages about a "good work ethic" were strongly reinforced.

Diane

Diane's father instilled in her a very strong belief in hard work. Her parents taught Diane that her value as a person was related to how much she accomplished, and she was raised to push herself and keep going no matter what challenges or obstacles arose. Until recently, Diane was unaware of how these parental messages negatively impacted her behavior and her relationships at work. In Diane's own words, "I am just beginning to see how I have taken on my Dad's messages. I never take sick time and I work long hours—I never give myself a break. I'm also beginning to understand why I'm so intolerant of my colleague, David when he takes time off to go fishing. It's hard for me to imagine sitting in a boat all day doing nothing! But now I'm learning that someone else could enjoy it and feel good about themselves because they received different messages. I'm starting to see how it is my beliefs that are creating so much tension in our relationship. I am also beginning to understand why people say I am hard to work for."

Remember, if you have a strong reaction to someone or something that shows up as a judgment or strong bias, you've probably triggered emotional patters from your cultural, religious or family values. Diane's new awareness about the effect of her upbringing on her current attitudes and behavior creates a new set of choices for her. Having identified her own biases as a driving factor in her perception, Diane can now make a choice. She can choose to see the situation not as "right" or "wrong," but as an opportunity to learn about herself and openly discuss her behavior with her co-workers. With this awareness, Diane's perceptual field is open and she can consider others' different perceptions without her emotional patterns causing judgments and defensiveness. We are not bad people because of our biases. Everyone has them and they will never go away. However, by being aware of our biases, we can identify and create new choices and behaviors for ourselves.

Move away from more than/less than

Often we rate people in relation to ourselves using a "more than/less than" scale. For example, we might think, 'He has more money than me', 'She's better looking than me', or 'I'm a better parent than they are—have you seen their kids?' We often do this from little or no information. **From a number of research studies, we know that it takes between 3 and 9 seconds to form a first impression of someone.** What are we basing this evaluation on? How much information can be accurately assessed in this amount of time? The answer is very little, if any, but we do it all the time. Think about the last time you had an empty seat next to you on an airplane, on a bus, or in a restaurant. As people came towards you and the empty seat next to you, did you have any preferences for which person sat down? If you're like most of us, you did. We size people up by instinct and "rate" them to get a sense of how we should relate to them.

Most of us strive to be "more thans." Striving to be a "more than" comes from a belief that our definition, status and power is found in things outside of ourselves like money, an important job, a big house, or other status symbols. We seek to acquire these things in order to feel good. A way to continue feeling good—to feel we are "more than"—is to have a lot of "less thans" around us because they confirm our more than status! Of course, this belief is erroneous. **We don't get our power from anything outside of ourselves, it comes from inside. And we all have the same access to it because it's the same power.** Yet, needing to compare ourselves, we construct worlds for ourselves where we star as "more thans". The more than/less than philosophy is often the foundation for entire organisations. We all know who the "more thans" are in an organisation. We tell from what floor their office is on, what their office furniture is like, how big their office is, whether they have a reserved parking space, or whether they can travel first class. These things in themselves are not the problem. The problem is that this leads some people—the more thans—to believe that they *are better and more worthy* than others, which often results in abuses of power and disrespect of the "less thans." We use words like 'equality' and phrases like 'valuing difference', but until we recognize and manage our own tendencies to rate people using a more than/less than approach, we will never move towards unity.

Notice the first thought and work on the second

Our childhood messages are very strong. So, even if we know what these messages are, and even if we want to change them, how do we do it? Consider this example from a woman in one of our diversity workshops.

Sara

Sara worked for a large company in London and was accustomed to seeing Muslim women dressed in their traditional shadors in various job roles within her organisation. Although she had many opportunities, Sara was never comfortable striking up a conversation with any of these women—specifically, the woman who worked as a cleaner in her office. Following the September 11 terrorist attack in New York City, Sara became more and more aware that she was avoiding having any contact with this woman. In our workshop, Sara was challenged to look at the thoughts that led to her avoidance or "flight" behavior. Sara noticed that her first thought was that the woman would not like someone such as herself—someone who was non-Muslim. When asked to focus on a second thought that would challenge the first, Sara realized that her first thought was an assumption—one not necessarily true and one she could set aside. Now that Sara clearly saw that her fear was driving her perceptions, she focused on what she would like to change. Sara also realized that she was curious about how the Muslin woman in her office was coping since the attack. If the woman seemed inclined, Sara decided to create a space for a conversation and connection with her.

Know you are *not* your patterns

Our past conditioning—our judgments, biases and emotionally triggered negative perceptions, are *not* the spirit and essence of who we truly are. **Our true identity rests in the peaceful knowing of our interconnectedness with all things.** This ongoing and deepening realization is the energy that vitalizes our ability to make true connections with people who are different from us. When our focus is on knowing and experiencing our true identity, our perception easily shifts and we can suddenly see the evidence to support this truth in others. The following story illustrates how this change in focus can create positive changes in the workplace.

Mike

Mike, a consultant, gave a presentation on diversity to a group of top civil servants in the United Kingdom. A key theme of the presentation was that effective diversity work begins by looking at ourselves first, and that if we have a problem with another person, this tells us more about ourselves than it has to do with the other person's behavior. After the presentation, one woman raised her hand and told Mike about a colleague in her team whom she didn't get along with, saying she found his behavior "obnoxious and inappropriate." She asked, "How do I deal with him? Do I have to accept him as he is because how I react to him is my responsibility?" The first part of her question was easy to deal with: no, we do not have to accept inappropriate behavior in the workplace. Organisations have policies and standards regarding what are acceptable and unacceptable behaviors, and how people are expected to contribute to the team, and how to act with respect. Mike encouraged the woman to utilize the internal resources in the Civil Service if she thought her colleague's behavior was outside these policies. The woman nodded, but Mike sensed that his answer wasn't really getting at her true concern. He asked her, "Is this about something deeper?" Does this have to do with how you feel about him as a person?" A little reluctantly and with a nervous laugh, the woman admitted, "Yeah, I really don't like this guy!" Everyone laughed, probably out of recognition for their own similar situations and feelings because, yes, there are people we simply don't like. Mike paused for a brief moment and told me later that he said the only thing he could. "You know, you are going to have see past the person he is presenting to you. He is not his behavior. The behavior he presents is not the truth of who he is. His behavior is just his past conditioning coming through, and does not represent the real person within. At the deepest level, we are all just possibilities coming into being, and we are all connected. He is a part of all of us, and we are a part of him. **You are going to have see beyond his behavior to the person he really is, and love him.**" There was a noticeable silence in the room and he continued, "It might help to remember that people who present themselves in this way are not usually in a good place. His emotional patterns may be deep and out of his awareness, and so he may be acting out of pain or fear, or both. Don't engage with him at the level of his behavior. Instead, see past his conditioning to the possibilities of love and goodness within him. Connect with him at this deeper level (you don't need to tell him what you are doing), and he will respond to you." No one laughed, jeered, or snickered and Mike reported that everyone looked thoughtful. What Mike did not say to the group was *why* this would work. **When we let go of our own conditioned responses and look past someone else's conditioning, we align ourselves with the quantum realm of all possibilities.** Shifts in behavior then happen naturally, and in sync with the fundamental laws of openness, connectedness and unity.

Break the ultimate pattern

If we are to be successful in creating new patterns, we need to learn how to let ourselves off the hook, and not beat ourselves up for our mistakes. It is essential to learn how to do this, because if we don't, we could sabotage all the other good work we are doing. What is doubly difficult is that we are the only ones who can do it! **We can ask for help, read guidelines, and hear other people's stories, but we are the only ones who can let ourselves off the hook.** It is a daily hour-by-hour activity; a continuous process of noticing how we put ourselves down, and affirming the truth that our essence is simply pure potential. Many of us are in deep patterns of guilt, fear, and shame, having received strong messages that there is something intrinsically wrong with us that needs to be punished. But this isn't the truth. These are merely patterns *and patterns can be broken*. By learning to recognize and break the ultimate pattern of beating ourselves up, the essence of our true self can flow through and create a change in our perception, and then a change in our experiences. Evidence of our own worth and lovability takes us into the new pattern of self-acceptance and self-love. If we create a fundamental pattern around self-acceptance and self-worth, then when we do revert to old patterns that we thought we had changed forever (and we will because it's simply the nature of the re-patterning process) we won't feel compelled to beat ourselves up thinking we failed in our attempts to change. **We need to be gentle with our-**

selves and be aware of our patterns, and not get hooked back into guilt and shame—the ego's lounge. Instead, we need to break the ultimate pattern and trust that we *do not have to do or prove anything* to be loveable in our eyes. It also happens that when we override the ego's assessment and see our selves as fundamentally good, it becomes easier to also see other people as essentially good, by assessing their motivations differently and assuming positive intent on their part.

4

Assuming Positive Intent

In the quantum realm, we have seen that everyone and everything is interconnected, and that at the most fundamental level, nothing is separate from anything
else. Within this unity, individual consciousness is simply an intention. **Whatever we set our intention on—consciously or unconsciously—is what will be
reflected back to us.** We see what we intend to see. All of our relationships are
mirrors, and whatever we see in another person is always a direct reflection of the
truth we hold about ourselves. Even when our intention is out of our awareness,
it is still directing our perceptions. As a result, we often unconsciously create situations that we believe we had no part in setting up. For example, when we are
really upset with someone, our reaction is usually happening on two levels. On
level one, there is the event or behavior that occurred that we didn't like or appreciate. But on another level, there are our beliefs and expectations about *the kind of
person who could have done this,* and these unconscious expectations and beliefs
impact the dynamics that get set in motion. Whether we are aware of our expectations and beliefs or not, they underlie our perceptions and drive our behavior,
and we end up creating situations that prove our point—oh, look what they've
done now—and the cycle continues. Unless we learn a strategy for interrupting
these unconscious expectations and beliefs we will find, with certain people in
particular, that no matter how hard we try to work things out on level one, we
still unconsciously mount evidence to prove that *they are the one at fault.* This
process keeps us stuck re-creating our past, and also prevents us from bringing
our own expectations and beliefs into the light so we can own them and alter
their affects.

Assuming positive intent is a tool that interrupts this process by deliberately
directing our intentions and beliefs about the other person. **Assuming positive
intent is witnessing the truth that at the most fundamental level each person
is simply pure potential, innocent and already whole.** When we intentionally
set our perceptions on this truth about a person, we simultaneously recognise this

37

truth within ourselves. By assuming positive intent, we open a space for each of us to experience a wider range of possibilities about who we are. At the practical level, assuming positive intent is simply the willingness to trust that the other person is doing the best that they can with whatever information and understanding they have at the time—no matter how illogical, weird, "stupid" or otherwise incomprehensible their behavior may appear to us. If they weren't doing the very best that they could, wouldn't they do something different anyway? **Assuming positive intent is about accepting someone exactly as they are—even if the behavior they are exhibiting is absolutely not the way we would choose to act.**

Accepting someone exactly as they are is not easy. It is especially difficult when our hard-wired patterns have been triggered, and we believe strongly that our negative attitudes and judgments are justified and reflect the total truth about the person. In this state, our emotional patterns will drive our perceptions, and we will look for, and find, confirming evidence for the person's flawed nature. When our perceptions are driven by our conditioned emotional patterns, it does not feel natural to question our assumptions about someone who we perceive as flawed, weird, stupid or aggravating. And yet, the truth is, whatever is unacceptable to us about them is just information about ourselves—our preferences and our own conditioning.

Assuming positive intent is a technique that helps us to create new habits and patterns in our most challenging and difficult relationships. Using this technique, we create the new habit of looking past someone's behavior to witness the truth about their nature. Assuming positive intent can feel odd the first few times, but with practice, we realize that by simply changing what we do first—assume positive intent—we create a positive shift in the dynamics of the relationship, even if the other person is unaware of the changes we have made.

Directing our intention

Our intention is a powerful energy. Assuming positive intent is a strategy for consciously aligning our intention with the fundamental laws of the universe. Aligning our intention in this way, we witness the deepest level of truth about a person—that at their core, they are already perfect and simply pure potential. Consciously aligning our intention with this truth about the nature of reality also aligns our intention with another quantum principle—that what we pay attention to is what we bring into existence. Deliberately directing a strong positive intention towards someone has the effect of shifting *our* perception, which then allows evidence of the person's unconditional worth to appear. When we hold the truth of someone's innocence and pure nature, *we* see them differently, and this changes what *we do next.*

Someone's behavior may be annoying, or even inappropriate, but perceiving the truth in them means that we have a choice about how *we* approach them. If their behavior is truly disrespectful, and it's having a negative impact, it needs to be addressed. However, holding the truth that they are simply doing the best they can, and letting go of our judgmental interpretations, sets up a dynamic of non-judgment in the communication process. **By shifting our intention, and seeing the other person's essence as loveable while we confront their behavior, we align ourselves with the unified field of all possibilities.** This frees us from hard-wired patterns, and frees the communication process from dynamics generated by fear, judgment, blame and punishment. When we truly shift our own perception, and witness someone's essence as pure potential, they can sense our non-judgment and are then more likely to hear about the affect of their behavior. Assuming positive intent then allows us to make deep and meaningful connections with whomever we want—regardless of our past conditioning.

If assuming positive intent is the way to open, honest, and respectful interactions, why is it so incredibly hard to do? Why is it so much more common to see people ascribing sinister motivations to each other, and assuming that their co-workers are working from a hidden agenda? One reason may be that people believe it saves them time and energy in the short term. Another reason may be that there *are* co-workers trying to get their own way at our expense. Yet, if we set our intention to automatically assume the worst of people, we will be protected and defended and never able to create any other pattern except that of reinforcing separateness by believing it is always others who are fault.

Our ego loves separateness. Setting up and nurturing a belief that others are acting willfully and intentionally to hurt us, creates a judgment of them that fires our anger and resentment, distorts our perceptions, and fuels the ego's desire for attack and control. When our emotional patterns are triggered, our perceptions get hijacked, and it becomes easy to believe that the negative things we see in the person are the only things that are true about them. Triggered emotional patterns constrict our perceptual lens, and the world starts to appear in terms of right and wrong, good and bad, win or lose—some of the ego's favorite hiding places. **Our triggered emotional patterns keep us stuck in the ego's illusionary world of separation and control.** Assuming positive intent helps us change our internal patterns by consciously focusing our intention and shifting our perceptions—which in turn, shifts the dynamics of the communication process.

Sometimes it may seem easier to not check our assumptions and not take responsibility for our reactions. But ultimately, operating from our ego not only keeps us in old patterns, but also sets us up to act as "more thans," taking a position of superiority that ultimately drains our energy. People in organisations who constantly defend a position of being "right" become stressed, tired, and less productive. Assuming positive intent brings about a huge positive shift in our own energy.

Still, when we are very upset with someone, it *is* incredibly hard to assume positive intent, and it is often the people in our immediate families and in our closest circles that trigger our hardwired patterns most intensely. Sometimes, the real difficulty with assuming positive intent lies not in applying the technique, but in our willingness to try it. Once we can find the willingness to try the technique, it can create a shift in the dynamics that brings about a transformation in the relationship. Consider the following story of Jenny and her brother Henry.

Jenny and Henry

Jenny was extremely mad at her brother Henry. Yet again, she found herself in a situation where she felt taken advantage of by him. This was a very old pattern that Jenny had learned to recognize a long time ago, but nevertheless, it was operating strong and it had Jenny in the throws of an extreme rage.

Much of the time Jenny could simply ignore what she saw as her brother's insensitivity and self-centered behavior. This worked unless they needed to discuss their mothers' health, and sharing responsibility for her care. This was exactly the situation Jenny found herself in now. Jenny resented her brother for not sharing this responsibility equally—especially since their mother had recently been ill and in hospital. Jenny absolutely detested her brother for not pulling his weight in this situation. After all, he lived closer to their mother than she did!

At these times, Jenny would find it almost impossible to have a reasonable conversation with her brother. She would get so incensed at his assertions that, "he was too busy," or "that his job was too demanding," that she would lose her temper, shout something sarcastic or mean, and then they would launch into a series of accusations and insinuations until finally one of them either hung up the phone or walked out of the room. It was just such a conversation that Jenny was re-playing in her mind as she drove to visit her brother. Once again, Jenny was going to try and speak with him about sharing their mother's care, only this time, Jenny really did want their interaction to be different. She wanted to have a conversation that was respectful and could also bring some resolution to the situation. Jenny wasn't at all sure it was possible, but she was willing to try the technique of assuming positive intent to see what might happen differently.

During the drive, Jenny found it very difficult to stay calm as she thought about her brother's behavior. At times she would completely abandon her willingness to assume positive intent, and find herself fanning the flames of her rage determined to let him know that his behavior was completely unacceptable, that he was an insensitive brute, and that he ought to start thinking of others besides himself! After all, isn't that just being completely honest with someone? Isn't that what all those assertiveness courses were about? Jenny even worried that if she just decided to love Henry for who he was and let him off the hook, she would actually be acting like a doormat and living in denial.

Jenny's strategy during the drive was to simply bring her self back into awareness of her thought patterns, and then repeat to herself, almost like a mantra, *"Henry is doing the best he can and if he could do it differently he would."* For the full hour's drive, Jenny vacillated between her fury and this technique.

When Jenny finally arrived at her brother's house, she knew for certain she wanted to try and be open to her brother's reality, and see the situation with their mother through his perceptual lens. She hoped this would have a positive affect on their interaction and their ability to come to some sort of resolution.

As a way of looking past Henry's behavior to see the truth about him, Jenny decided to focus entirely on Henry's perspective and his feelings, rather than on her agenda. Consciously shifting her intention to the truth that Henry is pure potential and doing the best he can at the level of his behavior, Jenny began to really look at her brother and take him in. As her intention became more conscious, she also noticed that she felt more of aware of the present moment, and that her expectations and resentments began to fade. As Jenny continued to look at her brother and hold him in this space of pure potential, she was suddenly struck by how tired he looked. Very sincerely and gently, Jenny said to him, *"Henry, you look very tired. Are things okay with you?"* Henry looked at her questioningly. Jenny could almost see the thoughts turning in his head—thoughts like, "Why are you acting so nice to me? What trick do you have up your sleeve?" For the first time, Jenny could see how little her brother actually trusted her to be even a little bit interested in him. Jenny found that very sad, and it caused her want to keep listening even more deeply.

As Jenny listened, Henry continued to talk more openly and honestly about himself. As Jenny learned more things about Henry's life that she hadn't previously known, the more she was able to set her judgments and resentments aside. Jenny learned some important things she had not known before. First, that

Henry's 25-year marriage was extremely strained and secondly, that Henry was suffering from an extended depression. Jenny's heart began to open as she allowed herself to enter Henry's world.

Jenny and Henry had a long, intimate conversation about Henry's current difficulties. Jenny helped Henry to think through some strategies for getting help for himself. In her whole life, Jenny had never had a conversation with her brother like this. She felt a renewed energy and connection with him. Jenny admired and appreciated his honesty and his vulnerability with her, and she found herself reinterpreting Henry's behavior around their mother. Jenny was beginning to realize that Henry could barely take care of himself, let alone someone else.

As the discussion returned to their mother's care, Jenny and Henry talked about some easy ways that Henry could support their mother. But even as they talked, Jenny knew deep down that his behavior was unlikely to change very much. Henry was simply doing the best he could. Whereas at one time, Jenny would have been contemptuous at worst, and pitying at best, she now recognized her brother's difficult situation, and was able to set aside her judgments.

In terms of Henry helping with their mother, Jenny realized she would still do for her mother whatever she could, and Henry would continue in his same way—being inconsistent and overly burdened by the whole thing. What had changed, however, was Jenny's resentment and anger towards Henry. Jenny no longer saw Henry as "the cause" of her pain. **She now had a completely different feeling about him—she could see both his potential—his lovability—and his limitations.**

So is this situation resolved? By shifting her perception of the whole situation Jenny changed in a big way. Jenny realized she could not control Henry or his actions, nor could she control or change her mother's loneliness or illness. With this realization, Jenny was able to go of her desire for control. In letting go of her brother and her mother's behavior, Jenny recognized that the only thing she could control, was her own reaction to all these things. Jenny felt a huge energy release as she gave up the notion that it was up to her to "fix" her family and orchestrate their behavior. In relation to her mother, Jenny discovered an additional shift in their relationship. She found that it was much easier to not react to her mother's criticism of her and the way she conducted her life. Jenny now was much more aware that she always had a choice.

At the start of this story, Jenny was completely focused on her brother's behavior, and her belief that he had fallen short of the mark. Jenny had momentarily fallen into the trap of seeing herself as a martyr—the magnanimous one who knew how to take care of their mother, and certainly a 'more than' in relation to

Henry's 'less than'. These perceptions fueled Jenny's resentment, inflamed her anger, and called up childhood memories that provided "evidence" to confirm her perceptions. But even in the middle of her deeply patterned and highly charged emotional patterns, Jenny was able to create a shift and get free by simply assuming positive intent and seeing the truth about Henry.

In terms of assuming positive intent, one or more of the following ego beliefs are likely to come up as the ego attempts to keep you locked in its world of control, distrust and separation.

Ego beliefs—Let Go's

"I know what's best for him/her/them"

I am so much wiser than this other person, and so it is my job to persuade them and get them to quickly agree with me. I have, after all, given this a great deal of thought. Wouldn't it be easier if they could just see how much I already know about the best way to proceed, and just let me handle it?

If we start from a position where we think we know best, it is very difficult to understand another person's position, or to be open to any solution they might suggest. When we remember that we are all connected, and pay attention to what the other person is saying, it often sets up a new dynamic that allows new information to show up that may change what the 'best' solution is.

"There is only one way to go forward and it's my way"

Having given so much thought to this situation, I have realized that there is only one solution—MINE. Otherwise, I would be suggesting different ones, but I'm not, I'm suggesting this one so why don't we just get on with it?

Apart from the countless family disputes that we may be involved in, there are also work and social situations where we believe that we are right, and we have absolute permission to take whatever measures are necessary to prove this to others—whether these measures are helpful and respectful or not. We have all seen professional adults resort to temper tantrums and backstabbing in order to get their own way. **Whenever you are preparing for a meeting in which you are seeking to convince, let go of the idea that your way is the only way!**

"Let me educate you so you will be wiser"

This is a very common "more than" belief. Because I have a lot more understanding than you, I am more than happy to be your teacher here. Once you have deferred to my wisdom and better judgment, then you can learn from me and soon you will be as wise as I am.

The belief that we are right, can lead us to act very patronizingly towards others who don't see things the same way we do, and the only patience we employ is waiting for them to concede. **It is impossible to assume positive intent if we start from a superior position.**

"It's up to me to figure it out because I care more, and understand all the people in the situation"

I have the ability to see this from every perspective, and I know much better than you, and I care much more for them, and so you should really trust me. I have taken it upon myself to put the time in and figure it out, so the least you could do is agree with me.

Many people who carry this belief will deny they do because it's not an easy thing to admit to. A good way to find out if you operate from this belief is to carefully observe your behavior when you feel strongly about something. Do you guilt people into agreeing with you? Do you shame and punish people in subtle ways until they cave in and let you have your way? These are all indicators that this kind of belief is driving your perceptions and your behavior.

"We can work on connecting *after* I've told you how to change."

The ego is constantly tempting us to look at people in terms of their shortcomings, and how they could be "better." When people don't meet our personal standards, we feel justified in judging them and seeing them as a "less than," and in need of some advice or feedback from us.

Thinking with any of these ego assumptions severely limits our potential to create the energy we need to deal with difficult situations. Keeping our hearts and minds open is challenging enough, but becomes even trickier by our belief that others need to be told *by us* what their problem is. Perceiving people's shortcomings, and holding these shortcomings as the truth, justifies our belief that others need to be more like us in order to be "worthy" of a connection. This belief bolts the door to our heart—as do all of the ego's beliefs. If we can let go of these beliefs, we at least have a chance of opening the door. Following are some key tasks that can help us develop the practice of assuming positive intent.

KEY TASKS

Enquire and listen to understand, rather than speaking from your own agenda

Assuming positive intent is about interrupting *our* hard-wired patterns of judgment, expectation and comparison, by letting the other person just be where they are, and then discovering how they see the world. If we are willing to listen deeply—past our own beliefs, values and standards—we will begin to see how their behavior makes sense to *them*. When we communicate with people at this level, it is always because one person in the encounter suspends their own preferred views of the world, and seeks to genuinely understand the views of the other—no matter how strange or uncomfortable the other person's behavior may have appeared. Consider the following conflict situation between two colleagues at work:

Ronald and Joanne

Ronald and Joanne were each assigned different parts of a research project. Completing their respective tasks did not require them to spend any time together, and so they only met up at the team meeting when it was time to present their findings. According to Ronald, the meeting did not go well. Ronald felt that Joanne continually tried to make herself look better than him. As Ronald recounted the events of the meeting to his friend Paul, he maintained that Joanne "dominated" the conversation in the meeting, and had acted "way out of line." Paul listened to Ronald's story, while reflecting on his own experiences with Joanne. Paul had worked with Joanne on and off for years, and never found her to be at all interested in her own success over someone else's. In an effort to help Ronald consider another perspective, Paul asked him two questions, *"What if you assumed positive intent on Joanne's part? What if you were to allow the possibility that she was acting from a completely different set of motivations than the ones you are convinced of?"* In that moment, Ronald did not think that Paul's questions were amusing. In fact, Ronald went away mad at Paul for not supporting him.

Later that day, Ronald found himself wondering why Paul, such a good friend, would have doubted his version of events. As Ronald calmed down, he began thinking about what Paul had said. Maybe he *had* misread Joanne's behavior. Ronald decided to have a conversation with Joanne. As they talked, Joanne laughed out loud and said "Ronald, I was not trying to set you up, I was trying to help you out. Every time there was an opportunity for you to present the details of your research, I would wait a long time for you to come in before jumping back into the conversation. When you didn't speak, I thought you were unprepared, or, just being weird." Ronald was taken aback, "No," he said, "I was very well prepared, and I wasn't being weird." I was just waiting for you to turn the agenda over to me, and when you didn't, I was so upset by what I thought you were doing, and what I was telling myself about your sinister motivations, that I didn't even see the opportunity to take over that part of the conversation."

After the meeting, Ronald began reflecting on some of the messages he had received as a black male growing up. Ronald wondered whether he would have been so quick to judge Joanne if she had been a black woman rather than a white woman. As a person of color, Ronald was beginning to realize that many messages of the messages he received as a kid about white women meant that he did not trust them very easily.

In this situation, Ronald went past his conditioning and his emotional patterning, and had the courage to check out his assumptions about Joanne—even though he had been taught to hold back. In his willingness to consider that maybe it was *his beliefs* about her behavior that were inaccurate, and that maybe it was *his* assumptions that were out of line, and *not her behavior*, he was able to learn something new about the situation and gain insight about himself. By simply suspending his initial hard-wired reaction, Ronald was able to enter into a conversation with Joanne and create an outcome that would not have been possible from the set of limited options his hard wiring offered. As it was, both of them were freed from a pattern of mistrust, anger and repeating their past.

Don't be defensive

It is easy to become defensive when someone gives us feedback about our behavior. Receiving someone's feedback is also a time when we are likely to fall into the fight or flight response and either become the aggressor—the fight response; or withdraw, close down, and become the victim—the flight response. As either the attacker or the victim, our defenses are up, and our perception is constricted as we focus on the "wrongdoings" of the other person. **When our perceptions are** driven by a fight or flight response, we cannot help but move into the role of victim or fighter—and in neither mode is our heart or mind open.

It is best to consider someone's feedback as a gift. When a person tells you something about yourself consider it gently. It may be a gift that fits—or—it may be someone trying *to make themselves comfortable* by focusing on changing you. Either way, be relaxed about other people's opinions of you. If the feedback makes you really angry, chances are it's true. Calm down, let it in, consider what is being said, and drop your defenses. An important part of assuming positive intent is to practice doing it in situations that would normally trigger our defenses. These situations are powerful opportunities to re-pattern some of our hard-wired conditioning—particularly the message that other people's opinions matter more than our own opinion of ourselves.

It is particularly difficult to drop our defenses when it is our boss or supervisor giving us the feedback, but it can still be practised and achieved. We can assume positive intent by taking the attitude that "this person has some things to tell me that I need to know so I can perform better, and they are probably nervous about telling me these negative things for fear that I will fall into the role of fighter or victim". By not reacting out of our fear, we can keep our minds open and notice a positive intent on their part. When we keep our defenses in check, it sets up a positive dynamic for the other person to do so as well. **Managing our defenses helps us to be able to use our intuition more effectively because we stay more connected to our calmer, more whole self.** Remaining in balance, with our intuition intact, also helps us to evaluate the accuracy of the feedback as well.

By not being defensive and assuming positive intent, we can change the dynamic, and the energy, and the meeting will contain a seed for something different and out-of-pattern to happen. Even though the words and the behavior of the other person might be harsh, our open minds will make it possible to see beyond the behavior to the essence of the person within.

By adopting any of the Key Tasks, in any of these situations, you will not only create the energy for making a true connection, but also generate energy that will keep *you* in harmony and peace—irrespective of what is happening around you.

See their behavior in their frame—not yours

According to Jenny's framework, Henry's behavior was unreasonable. She was looking at his behavior from her framework. She would have found it unacceptable to behave as Henry did. However, Henry saw it as not only reasonable, *but as impossible to do anything else.* If Jenny were to suggest changes to him, then the starting point would have to be where Henry is now, and not where Jenny is. By assuming positive intent, and really tuning in and listening to Henry, Jenny realized it was pointless to suggest any changes to him in that moment. It is always pointless to suggest anything to people that begins 'If I were you I would...'. We are not them, and whatever we suggest that might suit us, may be irrelevant, inappropriate, or even impossible for them to do. Once Jenny let Henry be who he was, and enquired why he felt the way he did, she experienced a completely different perspective, and had a different interaction with him. Let's see how seeing their behavior in their frame and not yours could be an effective strategy in a work situation.

Suppose you are a young female, and you have an upcoming meeting with your boss that you expect to be difficult because your boss doesn't share your family values. From previous interactions with your boss, you have learned that he doesn't approve of your lifestyle choices. As an older, traditional male, he doesn't like that you live with your boyfriend, and that you recently had a child together. But you love your job, and so you decided to shorten your maternity leave, and return to work early. When you informed your boss of your decision, he told you "not to worry," and that he "would arrange things so you could stay home for the full maternity leave, and not have to stress yourself and the baby." You informed your boss that wouldn't be necessary as your boyfriend was home full-time with the baby, and that everyone was happy and doing fine. Your boss remarked, "Sometimes there *are* things in life more important than work." In that moment, the tension was so thick, you decided to excuse yourself and calm down before trying to talk with him again.

Now, in order to make this next conversation an effective discussion, what are some typical strategies to consider? What are some common things we might be advised do to make this diversity discussion successful?

We can make a list:

- Let him know how you really feel.

- Tell him how his comment negatively affected you.
  Make the affect clear by being specific—both about the way you feel, and how it affects your energy, productivity, morale,
  respect for him, etc.

- Be sure and listen and empathize with his perspective

In diversity training, we emphasize the idea that for communication to be meaningful, each person must listen to the other deeply. The problem is, however, that we don't follow through with what listening at a deep level really involves. Rather than finding out about the person and what their life experience is about, we listen instead to determine if they heard *our points*. And often, as we tell them about their negative affect, our comments contain the subtle message that they are wrong. Who would want to listen to that anyway?

Everyone wants to be listened to in terms of *who they are*. When we really listen to someone without any expectations that *they* hear *us*, and really consider how it is in their world, the person will feel acknowledged and start wanting to hear us back. That is when real listening begins. So how do we apply this to diversity?

Consider now, that you are going to this next meeting with your traditional male boss. You have decided to try this Key Task and are going to "See his behavior in his frame not yours." So instead of spending a lot of energy thinking about what he said that you found offensive and hurtful, you simply note those things and set them aside. Next, you begin to consider everything in the situation from his perspective—who he is, what his life experiences have been about, and what might be some of the reasons why he made the comments he did. You allow yourself to really enter his world, and you begin to sense what it is like to be who he is. Some of the things you might see from inside his frame are that he is genuinely bewildered by the "new rules" that young people live by. What he grew up considering as "right" and "good" are no longer common norms in the workplace. Perhaps he doesn't even know how to relate to a young woman with so much independence.

Now, instead of taking the attitude: "I will let him know that his comments were offensive to me, and I will show him how professional I am, and insist he takes me seriously," you could adopt the following perspective: "He must be so confused about how to relate to women. Most of the women at work are nothing like his wife, and he is probably feeling very threatened by me. I think I will start the conversation by letting him know that I can understand his perspective. Instead of putting the focus on his offensive comments, I will put it on the fact that we are living with different values and ideas, and ask him his thoughts about that. I could start by sharing a time when I found myself challenged by change." By putting ourselves in the position of the other person's life experiences and listening from a place of interest and understanding, we set up a dynamic of trust and true respect. **When we establish a connection based on trust and true respect, we can then present our concerns about the work relationship**

within a context of appreciation and understanding. The tone and dynamics of the conversation go from "you need to hear how you did me wrong", to "I'd like to understand how you came to see the world the way you do, and I understand that if you could see the world differently, you would." By listening and really acknowledging *his* reality, it creates the space for him to care what his affect on you has been. With a trusting and respectful connection, it is much easier to share your concerns and requests in a manner that he will be more inclined to want to hear about and respond to. By changing *your* attitude before the meeting, you can create the energy that will allow a connection to be made. You will have changed the dynamic. What is so powerful is that assuming positive intent doesn't need both people to do it in order for it to work. Just one who is prepared to do it can change the whole relationship. Also, practising this technique has nothing to do with allowing yourself to be walked on, or not having your needs met. It is about opening the way to effective communication by being the one who is open minded and willing to listen first.

Choose compassion over judgment

Being willing to see life from the other person's point of view helps us to become more compassionate. Jenny's belief that Henry should have behaved more like her, led to her resentments and the triggering of her emotional patterns. In that state, Jenny's instincts did not lead towards understanding the situation from Henry's perspective. Compassion comes when we do the work to let go of our own resentment including expectations and assumptions. **Choosing compassion means that we keep our minds open, and accept the other person exactly as they are, without trying to change them into what we would like them to be.**

Don't try to change people—change your perception of them instead

At whatever stage of life we are, we carry a particular view of the world and how it should work. Whenever we find ourselves wishing the other person would change, we need to stop and consider our perception of them and the situation. In the following situation, a change in perception helped create a completely new relationship between Andrea and her mother.

Andrea and her mother

Andrea's mother had always been very critical of her, and continued to criticize her even though Andrea was now in her 40's, had a successful career, two happy teenage children and a 20 year marriage. Andrea's mother believed that Andrea was away from home too often, didn't look after her husband well enough, spent too much time on things unconnected with her family, was too old to dye her hair, and shouldn't work so hard because it meant she was neglecting her children—the list was endless. In her head, Andrea was forever screaming at her mother to accept her as she was, and to stop wanting her to be different. Time and again, as calmly as she could, Andrea would tell her mother that she was a wife, a mother, and a business woman; that her family was happy; that her kids were doing great; and that they were all leading full exciting lives—but her mother never heard her. Andrea was constantly caught between being irritated and angry with her mother, and yet wanting her approval.

Over the years, Andrea had tried many things to try and get her mother to understand her life, and give her some credit for all she had accomplished. And then one day, standing in her kitchen, Andrea felt a miracle happen. As Andrea stood crying and looking out the window after yet another difficult conversation with her mother, she had an incredible insight. **Andrea realized that while she was screaming at her mother to accept *her*, she was *not accepting her mother at all.*** Here was her mother with 80 years of life—and from what Jenny could gather, 80 years of disappointments and pain, including having a daughter who had not lived up to her expectations—doing the best she could. Andrea realized that she wanted her mother to be someone she could never be. Andrea had always complained, "if only she would accept me exactly as I am," and yet, she now realized that *she* was not at all accepting of her mother *exactly as she was.* So, right then, in her kitchen, Andrea decided to assume positive intent and accept her mother exactly as she was with her 80 years of pain, pleasure and efforts. Andrea decided to see her mother as doing the best she could. Andrea blessed her, loved her and vowed to let go of her expectation that her mother should be different—she was absolutely fine as she was. Andrea felt wonderful and a great peace descended on her. She told no one what she had done and went about her business.

The next day the phone rang, and it was her mother. This was very rare. Andrea's mother hardly ever phoned because she said, "I never know if you're going to be there." "Hi mum. How are you?" said Andrea. Her mother said, "I remembered you said you were working abroad this week. I just wondered how it had gone."

Andrea had to sit down. What had happened? In all of her adult life, her mother had never called her to chat about her work. **What had happened was that when Andrea changed her perception of her mother it changed the whole dynamic between them.** Although Andrea's mother had not been told what Andrea's thought process had been, somehow, at some level, she had felt the energy of connection that Andrea had created inside herself and responded to it. It is important to remember that Andrea did not do it to change her mother. She did it to bring peace to her own heart and mind. Yet, **by choosing peace and practising acceptance, Andrea brought about a change in the relationship that wasn't dependent on her mother changing.**

This is not a lesson that we learn only once. The fact that Andrea did this with her mother does not mean that she will never have to remember to do it again—especially when her mother is critical of her. However, each time she does it, it increases her energy and her skill at being able to manage difficult situations and relationships, and keep herself in balance and in peace.

We can practise changing our perception of people instead of trying to change them in a workplace setting as well—especially when we begin working with someone we are not automatically comfortable with. **It is important to remember that it is not someone's differences that act as a barrier—it is *our reaction* that gets in our way.**

When we feel uncomfortable, we often assume it is because of the other person. We want *them* to stop doing or saying what is that makes us feel uncomfortable.

We are not talking about unacceptable behavior like racist or sexist jokes, or threatening and abusive language. We are talking about someone acting differently than ourselves. For example, finding out that someone is gay; seeing someone who dresses differently than most others, someone who eats special kinds of foods, or someone whose accent is difficult to understand. Sometimes we aren't even sure what the difference is that causes us to feel uncomfortable, but there are countless examples of people whose differences act as a barrier because we believe it is something about them that needs to change. We want them to stop making us feel uncomfortable and change *their* behavior. By simply assuming positive intent, and doing any of the Key Tasks described, we can break through the barriers and ease the discomfort. In doing so, we are on the way to offering ourselves differently.

5

Offering Ourselves Differently

We spend a lot of time in organisations trying to get people to change. We send people to training programmes, we implement policies designed to alter their behavior, and we provide ongoing feedback in an effort to make people behave in ways we think they should. Yet, often all we really end up doing is creating employees who are compliant—employees who understand how to get along in the environment without getting punished. If we want to *truly* create change—and not just our surface behaviors—but our genuine ability to be authentically and truly ourselves—we must look at change from the perspective of the heart. **It is through our heart that we can offer ourselves differently, because it is our heart that authentically leads us into new patterns of love, appreciation, acceptance and joy.** Consider the story of Jane, a woman with a long of history of addictive behaviors who was finally able to change by finding the love within herself.

Jane

At 50 years old, Jane went into treatment for alcoholism. After completing the programme, Jane stayed sober for a little over a year and then returned to her old pattern of drinking. By the time she was 55, Jane had become very sick and was no longer able to work. Five years later, at 60, Jane went into treatment again, only this time she was able to stay sober for twelve years—until she passed away. Why was Jane able to stay sober the second time, but not the first? What makes such a huge shift in behavior possible? Perhaps no one knows all the specific elements that create such a transformation, but according to Jane, the most important thing she did differently was to accept the idea that love and gratitude are the basis of everything, and then surrender to this idea completely. Jane said that out of her complete desperation she became willing to give up her need for control, and she started focusing all of her attention on thoughts of love and gratitude instead. Through this process, Jane found herself becoming more open minded and willing to listen to other people's suggestions and ideas. She also found that her relationships with others were becoming easier and more filled with kindness and compassion. **Jane also found that by tuning into feelings of love and gratitude, she was able to more successfully sustain her new behavior patterns.** By listening to her heart, Jane discovered that she could offer herself differently in her relationships with others by letting go of the things she didn't like about people, and focusing on the things that she did like. This gave Jane new skills to be the kind of person she had always wanted to be. By using her heart as a guide, Jane was able to re-establish relationships with her children whom she had been estranged from for many years. Through her heart, Jane learned to access her own *internal experience of love and appreciation,* which then made it easier to express feelings of love, appreciation and joy towards others. After many years of estrangement and hostility, Jane's family had a number of connected and happy years together. How good it would be if we could learn to surrender to the experience of love and gratitude, and offer ourselves differently *before* we find ourselves desperate and in a traumatic situation. Our heart's intelligence often encourages us to open up and let go to this larger experience of love, but out of our fear, we resist this inner sense of knowing and put our faith in our mind's ego filled plans for control instead.

Over the past two decades, the mind/body connection has become an established medical fact. This established connection has been reported in magazine and newspaper articles all over the world, and it is now common knowledge that our thoughts and feelings directly affect our physical state, and our physical state directly affects our thoughts and feelings.

It is also well known that when we experience stressful feelings such as frustration or anger the nervous system is affected, and the stress response is activated. **Our feelings states are tied *so* directly to our nervous system and our neuropathways that even one minute of anger can cause a virtual cascade of physiological reactions.** This relationship between negative feeling states and our physiology has been well documented, and as we saw in Chapter Two, negative emotions hugely impact our perceptions.

But what is *also* true is that positive feelings directly impact our nervous system, our neurological pathways and our perceptions. **Just as in the case with anger, one minute of love or appreciation causes a virtual cascade of physiological reactions.** However, when we are experiencing positive feelings like love and appreciation, our physiology is *positively impacted,* and the nervous system becomes balanced, our heart rhythms form a coherent pattern, and the stress hormone cortisal is reduced while DHEA the youth producing hormone, is released. In addition, when we experience positive feelings, our perceptual field is opened rather than constricted, and our thinking processes become clearer and more efficient.

Let's try a simple experiment. Think for a moment about someone or something that you truly love and appreciate. Bring them into your mind. Now, pay attention to the feelings that are associated with this person or place. Just relax and *re-experience the feelings* as much as you can, letting them enter into your awareness while continuing to breathe gently. In doing this, you probably noticed a lot of subtle changes in your physiology. For many people, there is a quieting of the mind, and a sense of peace and contentment arises. Another common experience is to feel the breathing slow down, the muscles relax, and sense of well-being return. Many times people simply say, "I don't know, I just feel so relaxed and at peace."

It is generally assumed that positive feelings are something we have to earn—either from our hard work, or through approval from others. While these are definite sources of positive feelings, **it is important to realize that we can also intentionally generate positive feeling states in order to shift our physiology, and achieve a clearer, more compassionate and balanced perspective**. By shifting into positive feeling states, our perception shifts, and the evidence for a positive world appears. Learning to intentionally experience love, gratitude, appreciation and joy causes us to create more of these things in our world.

When we operate from love instead of fear, the body and the mind are balanced and we can then offer this self to others, bringing them into a balanced and harmonious interaction with us. When *we are* experiencing joy, appreciation and love, we bring this experience and its untapped possibilities into the dynamics of our relationships, and we find ourselves taking risks, and acting outside of our established pathways of fear and our need for control. Learning to shift our physiology is an important key to keeping our thoughts and feelings in balance, and learning to offer ourselves differently. In the following example, Martha finds herself operating from love and compassion, after realizing that her old hard-wired patterns were not helping her establish new ways of relating to her co-worker Gerald.

Martha and Gerald

Martha and Gerald work for the same technology-consulting firm, and sometimes make joint sales presentations. Martha does not enjoy working with Gerald. Martha's experience is that Gerald has a different set of rules and expectations for himself than he does for her, and that he is not open to receiving any feedback. For example, Gerald recently went way over his allotted time on the agenda, and when Martha confronted him about it, he said he had "very good reasons" for having done so. Gerald's response was, "The group needed more time to think through this part of the process." If it had been a reciprocal situation, it might not have created so much tension, but Martha had learned that if *she* went over *her* timeline, Gerald would criticize her and make sure to let her know how damaging it was for rest of the day's agenda. Also, giving feedback to Gerald about these kinds of issues never really helped the situation—he always had a list of reasons why he acted the way he did, and never demonstrated any interest in learning how his behavior affected her, or their working relationship. In fact, Martha had come to realize that giving Gerald feedback was a sure way of making the situation more strained and less resolved than it would have been had she said nothing at all.

Martha and Gerald were scheduled to co-present to a very important new client group. In getting prepared for the presentation, Martha decided she would focus on being as professional as possible. She told herself, "I am an adult, I can stay focused on the task and the group, and not let my irritation with Gerald get in the way of my doing a good job. I will put out the necessary energy to make sure that no one picks up that there is any tension between us." After rehearsing these thoughts, Martha felt sure that she could remain, calm, focused on the group, and respectful of Gerald's differences—at least to an outside observer. Even though it did take a lot of energy, she had certainly done it in the past.

Martha opened the presentation and everything seemed fine. She felt good about her work, and felt she had done a nice job setting the stage and creating positive expectations among the group. Gerald then began his part of the presentation, but instead of moving to the next item on the agenda, Gerald spent ten minutes re-stating the exact same points that Martha had just covered. Why did he do this? Hadn't she just handled all those same points? What was he trying to accomplish? Didn't her input count? She felt her heart rate begin to rise.

Martha watched the lightning-quick process with which her judgments took hold and dominated her view of the situation. **As her mind flooded with negative thoughts, Martha remembered other times with Gerald where similar things had happened, and her perceptual lens began to narrow.** In that moment, Martha believed, without a doubt, that Gerald was absolutely *"wrong"* and *"should"* have acted in a way different from the way that he did. The power of these emotional thought patterns also left Martha very angry and feeling stuck.

As she started to calm herself, she realized she was in a no-win situation. She could either give Gerald feedback and get slammed by him again, or she could continue carrying this incredible energy of judgment while pretending nothing was wrong. In this extremely uncomfortable place, Martha decided to try something different. She decided to try and use her heart rather than her head to guide her thoughts and perceptions of Gerald.

Martha began to slowly shift her awareness, and to purposefully use her intention to bring herself into a positive feeling state. She took a deep breath, and began to focus on the things in her life that she loved and appreciated. Activating these feelings began to balance Martha's physiology, and as her physiology became more settled so did her thought patterns. As Martha continued to focus on feelings of love and appreciation, the easier it became for her to let go of her negative, judgmental thoughts about Gerald. It was almost as if her thoughts became neutralized and less charged. Martha began to experience a noticeable change in her perceptions, and she started to consider the situation through a more loving and compassionate lens. As she sat to the side of Gerald and watched him, Martha began to notice things she had never seen before. She noticed how scared Gerald was, and how much he wanted the group to like him. She saw how much energy he put into his stories and examples, and how seriously he took everyone's questions. Mostly, Martha noticed how much—in his own way—he was trying to do a really good job. Suddenly, Martha realized that all her judgments of Gerald were about things that simply made him human. When Gerald's behavior began to appear in this light, Martha was able to see his spirit and recognize how much he was exactly like herself and everyone else—human, flawed and loveable. Martha was amazed at the shift in her energy. After the presentation, she decided to tell Gerald some things he had done well during the presentation—some things that she genuinely liked. He looked at her rather strangely, but he could also see that she really meant it. Martha smiled at him genuinely and happily, content in the realization that it was now possible for her to manage her relationship with Gerald differently. **Martha was clear that she could continue to create understanding and appreciation of Gerald within herself as long as she kept her heart as her guide.** Martha may never be motivated to develop a friendship with Gerald, but she was now able to work with him in a way that generated positive energy for *herself* as well as for the situation. Also, it is possible that Martha's creating positive energy patterns will shift the dynamics of the relationship enough for trust to develop. Once there is a small amount of trust and some form of connection, Gerald may even be able to hear Martha's feedback, and they may each have the opportunity to learn and grow from the relationship.

The heart keeps us in our integrity

Integrity is both the ability to do the right thing *and* the ability to know what the right thing is to do. In the corporate world, we see situations every day where people compromise who they truly are—not giving voice to their most creative ideas, withholding their most deeply held feelings, or not pursuing their most cherished aspirations—because they feel that the environment is not safe and won't support such unique aspects of themselves. It's true—the environment is not safe a lot of the time. Whenever we reveal our true selves and act in ways that are not the norm of those around us, we subject ourselves to the possibility of ridicule, judgment and worse—out and out retaliation.

In the ego's world of competition, attack and defend, we are always going to be the object of someone else's desire for control, or their manipulation for getting their own way. When people act in these ways, it is simply because they are operating from the ego and not from their heart—their compassion and love. When someone is playing political games and trying to control outcomes, misrepresenting the facts for their own gain, or lying to cover their mistakes, it is the ego asserting itself and trying to convince us that our security lies outside of ourselves. The heart represents the center of who we are, and in consciously creating feelings of love and appreciation we come closest to experiencing the essence of our truest self. **If we learn to tune in and listen to our hearts, we will be guided to act in ways that are not about playing ego games.** We will receive clear guidance and have the courage to act on our insights and remain in our integrity. How many of us have gone along with something at work even though we felt it was a wrong decision, or at the very least, made us feel very uncomfortable? How many of us have stayed silent when a sexist joke was made, when someone was ridiculed or humiliated, or when a decision was made that we did not agree with? It takes courage to step forward and say "I feel very uncomfortable about this." Having the courage to act with integrity can inspire others to do the same. It isn't always easy to act with integrity, but it is essential in this new framework we are building. Organisations will change only when the quality of our interactions change. In offering ourselves differently, we appreciate and utilize our powers of reason, but we check to make sure that our heart—our compassion—is also engaged. By learning to create a link between our hearts and our heads we stay in touch with what is true and integral for us.

Operate from love not fear

A consultant we know was working with a group of executives helping them create more respectful working environments within their organisations. As a part of the learning process, the consultant gave each of the executives a topic to research in their own operational areas, and they were then asked to bring back examples for the next week's meeting. One of the questions in the assignment was "Where does love show up in your organisation?" As the female sales director looked at this particular question, she rolled her eyes and groaned, "Give me a break—what has love got to do with business?" The consultant acknowledged that this was not a routine question, but asked the group to consider it anyway. The consultant then asked the whole group to reflect on whether they had seen any examples of love in their meeting that day. After some nervous laughter and a few jokes the examples started to come forth:

- 'You asked me how my wife was'

- 'You offered to copy me a document'

- 'You got me a coffee'

- 'You gave me a beaming smile when I came in'

- 'You congratulated me on last month's figures'

The Sales Director was intrigued, but skeptical. She conceded that there had been some "nice pleasantries" in the room, and admitted these things do help people feel connected and positive, but she said, "these things are not love." It is true that the word "love," when used in a work context makes many people nervous. Many people feel that using the word love is very inappropriate in a corporate setting—even risky. It is interesting to note that in the workplace, there is a much stronger taboo around talking about love than there is around discussing hate. We use the term hate all the time, and without blinking an eye, we deal with the myriad of difficulties that come directly from people hating each other in the workplace. But what if it were okay to talk about love? What if we invested the same amount of energy in conversations about increasing the amount of love as we do about reducing the amount of hate? We can define love in a number of different ways—being open to really connecting with someone, being thoughtful, showing concern toward someone, saying thanks, seeing beyond someone's behavior, spending time listening to someone, or telling someone what they did well. Even though these are small acts they are all extensions of love. What if we could explicitly acknowledge the fact that love is a fundamental psychological need of every human being, and that when we receive love, we feel more settled in our own truth, and more able to concentrate and apply ourselves? In our experience, many people in the workplace are ready to acknowledge the power of love and how it works because they are so tired of the old way.

It is helpful to remember that operating from love simply means making the decision to see what is good and positive and life giving. When we make this decision—and we have to make it several times in a day—we align ourselves with a perception that mirrors the truth that we are already interconnected and a part of each other. When we choose this perspective, we engage new patterns of acceptance and we reflect openness while our work environments become more naturally inclined towards respectful encounters.

Jamal and Derek

Jamal, was a participant in a diversity training programme. During one of the breaks, Jamal asked Derek, the facilitator, to help him with a situation concerning his boss. Jamal told Derek that at the time he was hired, he was told he would become a group team leader within three months. Jamal said that it had now been five months, and he still hadn't been offered the position. He told Derek that when he recently asked his boss about the position, he was given reasons that seemed vague and were very hard to understand. As he spoke, Derek could see that Jamal was visibly upset. Derek asked Jamal if he thought he was being discriminated against. Jamal looked at the floor for a long time and said, "Yeah, I do, the guy is always saying negative stuff about foreigners when he thinks I can't hear him". Derek reflected on how painful it feels to be treated negatively and unfairly. He then asked Jamal if he wanted to confront his boss about the situation. Jamal said that he did. Derek put his hand on Jamal's shoulder, and told him he would support him in any way he could. Derek tuned into his own heart, and was guided to ask Jamal another question. Gently he asked Jamal, "Is there anything that you *do* like about this job or this company"? Surprised at first, Jamal replied "Yeah, there are a lot of things I really like about this place—that's what makes it so hard." Derek then asked Jamal to consider going forward using his heart to help him keep things in perspective. He acknowledged that Jamal's anger was completely justified, and asked to him to also consider not letting his anger drive all of his perceptions. Derek asked Jamal to consider keeping his heart open, and to allow some of what is good about the company to be a part of his awareness. Derek explained that this would help him stay in balance, and open the possibility for something good to come out of the situation. Jamal looked doubtful. "Okay, he said," and they shook hands. Reflecting later, Derek hoped that Jamal would try some of his suggestions, and *discover for himself* that he could both be angry and challenge the system without having to become a victim. If Jamal could maintain even a small degree of openness about the situation as he went through it, he could mitigate the emotional patterns associated with being a victim, and lay the foundation for something new and positive, and completely out of pattern to occur. If Jamal could begin with what he appreciated in the situation—the things he liked about his job and the organisation—he would be able to act with a more loving and heart-centered approach. One of the easiest ways to offer our selves differently, and activate more love in the workplace is to start from appreciation. So how do we do that?

Start from appreciation

There are a million things we could appreciate—even when things are difficult. All we have to do is be willing to notice them. Wherever we put our attention will drive our experience. If we look for things to appreciate and be grateful for, we can find them.

The world is filled with incredible beauty. Each of our lives contains magnificent places of natural splendor, an array of fantastic people, and incredible symmetry and serendipity—that is, if we choose to notice it. Often times we don't. Given all the crime and atrocious acts committed every day, it is easy to see the world as a scary and negative place. But why do we focus on the horror so much of the time? What if the news media spent one week reporting *only positive news,* and bombarded us with only positive images and ideas about our greatness as a species? Wouldn't we end up with a strong, positive perception of humankind and our world? Offering ourselves differently is about being courageous enough to hold this perception for ourselves—even when others choose to see only the negative. We can create the feelings inside ourselves *irrespective of what is going on outside.* We can find the beauty and the potential for openness and love at any time and in any place. And acting with a willingness to see the beauty brings a new quality to whatever task we are doing and to every interaction we have. A willingness to see what is positive in a situation creates a space for love and open-heartedness to enter. This feeds our energy and allows us to reach out and stimulate the energy growth of others. **We are the participants in the reality that we create, and so whatever perception we choose, the evidence to support this**

perception will always appear. If we are addicted to misery we will always find things to be miserable about and people to blame for our unhappy state of mind. Keeping our senses open, and noticing and appreciating things will help to keep our hearts open, and will create the space for joy and gratitude to enter our lives and flow freely.

We need to see *our own* magnificence

Did it make you cringe to read that? How many times do we deflect a simple compliment? Instead of just saying "Thank you," we say, "Oh—this old thing, I've had it for SO long," or "I'm not sure it's really my color ", or "Oh, don't worry, it wasn't that much work," (after we stayed up all night doing it). Many of us find it difficult to accept even a simple compliment because we aren't in touch with the truth about ourselves—that, at our core, we are pure and magnificent potential. Like all of nature, we exist as seeds coming into being. Our true magnificence comes out of our interconnectedness with all things, and the truth that all of reality—including us—is simply pure potential. It is the ego that is so concerned with living up to others' expectations, and trying to prove our worth. The ego's notion is that we are unworthy until proven otherwise. The essence of our true self is just the opposite. In our true essence, we are bright and worthy and magnificent. However, it is often the ego's voice that dominates, and we fail to hear the softer voice of love and compassion that shows us this deeper truth about ourselves. To ensure its dominance, the ego wants us to be afraid of these deeper truths. And yet, if we don't challenge these ego messages, we wind up afraid of own inner strength, beauty and power—our own magnificence. **Each one of us has a magnificence that would shine from us—if only we would not hide it.** Marianne Williamson, in her book, *Illuminata: A Return to Prayer,* says it well:

> *Our deepest fear is not that we are inadequate.*
> *Our deepest fear is that we are powerful beyond measure.*
> *It is our light, not our darkness, that most frightens us.*
> *We ask ourselves, "Who am I to be brilliant, gorgeous,*
> *talented, and fabulous?"*
> *Actually, who are you not to be?*
> *You are a child of God.*
> *Your playing small doesn't serve the world.*
> *There's nothing enlightened about shrinking so that*

other people won't feel insecure around you.
We were born to make manifest the glory of God
that is within us.
It's not just in some of us;
it's in everyone.
And as we let our own light shine, we unconsciously
give other people permission to do the same.
As we are liberated from our own fear,
our presence automatically liberates others.

As we move into the Let Go's for this chapter, just an additional word of caution. The ego will have a field day with the ideas in this chapter. Remember, the ego is heavily invested in projecting an *external image* of importance that keeps us in a "more than" position, and everyone around us in a "less than"' position. Seeking a connection with our true *internal magnificence* is actually threatening to the ego. The ego knows that once we start offering ourselves differently by creating new patterns based on internal magnificence, it will have less control over our perceptions and our actions. Remember, the ego is just a pet dog, and so smile at your ego, pet it, and then choose to offer yourself differently. Over time, we learn to create rich relationships filled with differences and meaningful connections. So if we are to offer ourselves in the ways outlined here, what ego beliefs do we need to let go of?

Ego Beliefs—Let Go's

"The world is a scary place, and I need to be worried or I won't be prepared"

Absolutely, the world is a scary place—to the ego. At any moment, the ego can be robbed of its security and made to feel stupid, misunderstood or otherwise threatened. We are not our egos. At our essence, we are connected to the unified whole, and this self can never be threatened because it is not based on anything conditional—it rests on our own inner perceptions of love and acceptance. It is a fact that there is no security outside of ourselves—we could lose our job any day, the people we love will get hurt, we will make some bad business decisions, friends and loved ones will die. These are all things that will happen to us, but if we worry as our primary coping strategy, we will also be engaging our negatively patterned neuropathways and perceptions. Choosing to offer ourselves differently does not mean that we stick our heads in the sand and not deal with the frightening and often traumatic facts of our lives. In offering ourselves differently, we choose to engage our patterns of love, kindness, care and consideration, allowing these to balance our perceptions *as we go through life's difficult and scary situations.*

"It sounds like we are supposed to be robots"

The point is not that we shouldn't get upset because we will! At times, we *will* find ourselves drawn into a dramatic whirlwind where the facts of a situation trigger our conditioned patterns of fear, and we have an emotional freak-out. The point is, when we find ourselves in a situation where our emotions are running high, we need to recognize where we are, and do what is necessary to *deal with and release the emotional energy first.* Whether we call a friend, have a good cry, go for a walk, throw something at the wall, or make sarcastic jokes with a friend, we do it as a *conscious* act of releasing the emotional energy. **As we settle down, we then begin looking at how our perceptions are fuelling the situation, and we begin taking responsibility for them.** Once we are clear about how our patterns and beliefs are operating, we can then look at the situation with clarity and engage the heart. By engaging the heart, our patterns of love and appreciation will bring our perceptions into balance. We can then be guided in determining the best actions to take, or whether any action is even necessary. The more we practise this, the more we begin to see how many times these "dramas" are simply monsters in our own minds.

"If we choose to just love and accept ourselves then we are operating in complete self-delusion"

The ego loves this position. To the ego, making a mistake means being "wrong" or "bad," and becomes the proof of our unworthiness and our need to be punished. The ego wants us to believe that we are comprised of only these dynamics so that we get tied to a never-ending cycle of being "wrong" and needing to be "punished." Here we get caught in the ego's web of riddles because if I am the person who committed the "wrong," how can I also be the person to forgive myself? And if we aren't connected to the inner part of ourselves that is capable of releasing us from this perception, we become like frantic hamsters on a wheel of doubt, self-loathing and fear. We remain at the mercy of the ego's crafty "proof" of our basic unworthiness, and our mistakes and shortcomings provide ammunition for the ego's belief that we don't deserve to be let off the wheel. Through its dedicated belief in our worthlessness, the ego attempts to keep us hostage to self-hate, and unaware of the real truth about ourselves—that we are magnificent at our core, *and* that we get to make mistakes as we learn to realize our potential. The ego likes to keep us stuck in the belief that we need to be punished because this keeps our fears about ourselves alive and real, which often triggers the additional limiting belief that bad stuff happens to us because we deserve it. Hence, we never attempt to connect with the love and pure potential that lies within, or experience the essence of who we truly are. **When we learn to offer ourselves differently, the ego's "evidence" of our basic unworthiness is replaced with the inner experience of the heart's knowing that we are actually made of love.** In this experience of ourselves as love we see clearly that we are not separate egos. **By shifting this basic perception about our selves, we create a different reality and, experience ourselves as a part of all things and connected to the whole.**

"But I've still got problems and I shouldn't have should I?"

There will always be difficult situations and people that we find really hard to deal with. We are not suggesting that our lives will become conflict free once we have established new patterns and learned to offer ourselves differently. This is not about creating a perfect life—it's about dealing differently with the life we have.

So, what are the key tasks we can identify to help us in offering ourselves differently?

KEY TASKS

Have a clear statement of intent

In his book, *The Hungry Spirit*, respected British consultant Charles Handy states:

> *"To be Properly Selfish is to accept responsibility for making the most of oneself by, ultimately, finding a purpose beyond and bigger than oneself."*

From an early age, most of us are taught the importance of setting goals and establishing specific plans for achieving them. This is good advice. The problem is that we get caught up in our goals, and we lose our inspiration and the meaning and purpose behind what we do. We begin to get lost in the constant struggle to achieve our goals, and we also get incredibly attached to specific outcomes.

Having a clear statement of intent is making a declaration from our deepest and most authentic self as to what our purpose is really about. This can be a simple statement that we craft, or it can be a few lines from a poem or book. But it is something that deeply represents to us, who we are at our core, and how we want to live as a result of this knowing. Once we have a statement of intent that clearly reminds us of why we are here and what our true self is really about, we can then use it to keep ourselves from getting lost. We can lift our focus to this larger blueprint, and remember the truth of our inner essence, whatever moment we are in. We can stay in touch with the reasons why we want to offer ourselves differently, and be more in touch with the process as it unfolds. A statement of intent acts as a compass letting us know where to make corrections and adjustments in our behavior and our decisions, and when we are off course, we can bring ourselves back without engaging in self-judgment or blame.

Work from your highest thought

Take a moment to think about how you would describe yourself when you are completely "on form." When you are at your best, what are you like? Would any of these things describe you: energized; connected; inspirational; motivating of those around you; capable; fearless; creative; loveable and loving? Now, ask yourself, when you are at your *worst* what negative beliefs are operating? Would it be anything like these: I don't really deserve to be totally happy; I must earn the right to be loved; I need to pay for my mistakes in suffering and pain; if I make a mistake, everyone will reject me; I have very little of value to offer to anyone. We all possess both the capacity to see our own magnificence, and the tendency to get caught in our negative belief loops. At times, we feel confident and at peace with our positive qualities, and yet at other times, we are caught in the ego's perception and buy into the belief that we are not good enough. **What we need to remember is that our most negative belief is the lie—it is not who we are—it is who we are not. We always have a choice**. If we are caught in a negative thought loop, we can go to our heart and remember the truth of who we really are, and then change our inner self-talk to match the feeling of this truth.

Watch your language!

We can choose to operate from our highest thought by paying attention to the language we use about ourselves. And if we are serious about seeing our magnificence, then it is important that we watch the language we use on a daily basis. When we scream at a driver who cuts us off in traffic, it triggers *our* stress hormones and negative patterns, *not theirs*. Our cells and nueropathways don't know we are talking to someone else! It is also important to become aware of how we talk to ourselves. How many times a day do we fall into the trap of negative self-talk by calling ourselves stupid? How often do we complain that we are fat? We must just stop it! Instead, talk to yourself in glowing terms. Tell yourself all the things that you wish someone would say to you. **Offering ourselves differently involves creating new patterns within our selves—patterns that then support and sustain love and acceptance in our relationships with others.**

See something to be grateful for in every situation

This is not easy, as some situations are obviously difficult and painful. Jamal will probably not have an easy time confronting his boss and standing up for what is right, and we would not expect him to approach the situation in a complete state of gratitude. Yet, he can keep an awareness of something positive that could come out of the situation if he were willing to see it. Bringing ourselves back to gratitude and looking at situations in terms of what they might offer us also helps us to see the meaning and purpose in the events of our lives. Focusing on gratitude, we learn to trust that every situation holds a gift for us—and in looking for it—the gift will appear. It may not appear immediately, but all that's necessary for us to find it, is our willingness to see it. It may come as an insight, a new understanding about ourselves, or learning we can apply to prevent us from getting in that situation again. **Regardless of what the gift is, finding it can help us to move on from the pain of the situation.** Another thing that can help us keep our focus on gratitude is to remember that we *only have absolute control* over our selves and our own reactions. We have no control over what happens to those around us. That doesn't mean we do nothing, just that we need to start consciously choosing our reactions. **By taking our focus off others, and putting it on our own reactions, we can notice the gifts embedded in the situations of our lives—even the difficult situations.** If there is only one thing you remember from this book—make it consciously choosing your reactions!

Actively seek connections with others

We are naturally drawn to people with whom we think we might have something in common. This impulse to connect leads us to favor people who look familiar—people we've had the experience of connecting with in the past. When we see someone who has a difference with which we are not familiar, we are less likely to make the effort to approach them and try to establish something in common. Suppose you had three minutes to find as many things as you could in common with someone you don't know very well, or you assume you don't have much in common with. You can include anything from shoe size to favorite wine, to where you grew up, to the number of grandparents alive, to your values and beliefs. In three minutes you are likely to find at least one thing you can connect about, or you might find twenty or more things! **The point is, we all share the experience of being human and if we look for it, we can always find a place to connect with someone about this shared experience.** Our humanness might look different—it might come with an accent, a different style of dress, or a different sexual orientation, but the shared human experience is always there if we open ourselves up and see it. We can then extend this recognition to another person who is very different, and make a connection. Paradoxically, finding how we are connected often leads us to appreciate someone's differences even more. **The reality is that we begin to make a connection with people when we open our hearts.**

Listen differently

Previously, we talked about listening as an important of part of assuming positive intent. Listening is also an important part of connecting with people and offering ourselves differently. We can listen on three different levels—listening to the words, listening for the feeling behind the words, and then listening *for what is really going on.* It is at this level of listening that we can really learn something about how a person experiences their world. In offering ourselves differently, we listen at this level by using our hearts, and by putting ourselves in another person's situation with compassion. Listening at this level, we might detect that someone is speaking from a negative belief about themselves, or from their greatest fear. When people say, "He really heard me," or, "I felt really heard," what is it they really mean? They mean that someone listened beyond the obvious, and tuned in to their deepest desires and concerns. One of the greatest gifts we can give to someone is to really hear them. **When we connect with what someone's** deepest self is saying, the energy of that connection is extremely powerful and can open new paths for both parties.

Be open to each moment

By noticing things we appreciate about ourselves, and about others and our environment, we set the stage for connections to happen easily and in unexpected ways. Staying in appreciation helps us to discover the connections possible in every moment. In fact, we begin to expect connections to happen at any time, and at any place. We have all experienced the wonderful serendipity when something unexpected happens and then realize it was meant to be. Perhaps we hadn't planned to be at a certain place, but when we got there, we met someone who turned out to be a significant person in our lives—or they had something important to tells us. These kinds of serendipitous connections are always possible—all we have to do is begin to look for them. As we continue these practices, we will begin to see that there are always clues available in the present moment—we just need to watch for them *and not be surprised.* At these times, we can really appreciate the truth that things interconnect in the present moment. **By staying present and open to each moment, and the connections and possibilities it contains, we become awake to our unfolding future. Staying open to the present moment also helps us discover feelings of kindness, grace and joy within ourselves, and to be more receptive to others.**

Ask for guidance

Even though we are committed to offering ourselves differently, we might find that some of our patterns are hard to break free from. When this happens, we can ask for help and guidance. You may believe in a God you can ask, or you may believe in a Guardian Angel or Spirit Guide. Call it what you will, the important thing is to be willing to ask for help from something outside of the ego. The willingness to let go of what we think is "right" or "best," and the specific expectations of our own progress allows us to move into the larger rhythms of the universe. **When we shift into a place of asking for guidance, we let go of our own ideas about how things should be, and develop the ability to trust the process as it unfolds naturally and in its own time.** The process of letting go is what matters; not what we use to help us do it. Asking for guidance and letting go develops our ability to listen and discern the subtle messages that come from our intuition and our hearts—information that is tied directly to our most essential and true selves. Sometimes we just know what to do or say before we have even worked it out, and learning to ask for guidance is a great practice for developing this ability to generate intuitive information in the moment.

For example, suppose we are faced with an important decision, but we are unsure of which direction to go. We could do what we have always done and use *only* our minds to list the pros and cons, benefits and barriers, and evaluate all the options. Or, we could set aside our analysis for a moment, and ask for guidance. We can learn to ask, "Is this really what I should be doing right now? Is this in line with my statement of intent?" Then based on this intuitive information, we can correct our course of action. It is a challenge to balance analytical thinking with learning to listen to our inner voices of guidance and intuition, but with practice we discover that our hearts direct us towards open-mindedness, creativity and willingness to go past our ego inclinations. With practice we also learn to trust that we *will* get an answer—even though we don't always like what the answer is! Sometimes we doubt the answer and then realize—usually too late—that we should have followed the guidance! Discerning intuitive guidance is a learning process. A helpful tool is to ask yourself if your intuitive guidance is asking you to go past your pride or give up some other ego attachment. If the answer is yes, chances are the guidance is helpful and you are simply resisting. Once we learn to ask for guidance and to trust that guidance, we realize that we have so much more energy—energy we used to spend trying to control and work things out.

Celebrate yourself—show your true colors

A big part of offering ourselves differently is to learn to be who we are, and not be afraid to have fun with our differences and take risks in connecting with others. Some people might think that offering ourselves differently is about being passive and boring. Just the opposite is true. When we show our true colors, we stand up for what we think is right, and we do it in ways that are inclusive and create interest and energy. **Offering ourselves differently means connecting with others to discover who we might be together and allowing our true selves to show.** We are not seeking balance and harmony that is quiet and subdued—we are looking to connect in ways that create sparks setting off small fires, but to do it all with respect and from a position of love and integrity. Offering ourselves differently, and operating from a place of openness and love becomes easier once we realize that we are already the people we have been waiting for everyone else to be.

6

We are the people we've been waiting for

When I let go of what I am, I become what I might be.

—*Lao Tzu*

The emphasis in this book is on taking individual responsibility by creating *The Energy of Connection* within ourselves. We have seen how perception creates *our* reality, but is not *the* reality. We have seen that to truly appreciate and connect with others, we need to learn to shift our ego driven patterns of separation and control that are embedded in our physiology. And it is by offering ourselves differently that we can create new patterns—patterns that arise out of perceptions based on love and appreciation. Through these new patterns, we align ourselves with the underlying principles of unity, wholeness and the field of all possibilities, and become inspired participants in the creative unfolding of our lives.

Any successful diversity effort within an organisation must recognize this power of individual perception. The individual always has a choice—not about *what* is happening to them—but about how they want to *react* to what is happening. A successful diversity effort will only effect real change when it recognizes that perception and individual reactions are essential to unlocking conflicts and transforming them into opportunities for creative outcomes. **Diversity training initiatives won't give people opportunities for real change without a corresponding emphasis on the nature of reality and the power of perception.** Unless people understand that the events they encounter are their opportunities for transformation, they miss the opportunity to align their conscious intention with the unity and wholeness that is already there. Without this conscious intention and alignment, change is undertaken with the false hope that resolution will be acheived by getting some else to change their behavior.

Unity not separation

In the past few decades, numerous physicists and lay people have written about the profound similarities between the findings of the New Science—Quantum Physics—and writings from ancient mystical texts. All major religions—Christian, Hindu, Buddhist, Jewish, and Muslim—have produced mystics who describe their direct experience with the nature of reality as that of "oneness," and who express a profound awareness that there is no separation between ourselves and the outer world. If we focus on the truths contained within these religions, we learn about our similarities and our unity. Caroline Myss, in her book *Anatomy of the Spirit*, writes:

> *"The truths contained in the scriptural teachings of the different religious traditions are meant to unite us, not separate us. Literal interpretation creates separation whereas symbolic interpretation—seeing that all of them address the identical design of our spiritual natures—brings us together. As we shift our attention away from the external world and into the internal one, we learn symbolic sight. Within, we are all the same, and the spiritual challenges we face are all the same. Our external differences are illusory and temporary, mere physical props. The more we seek what is the same in all of us, the more our symbolic sight gains authority to direct us."*

Similarly, Quantum Physics demonstrates that the universe is a dynamic web of interconnected and inseparable energy patterns, and that there is no such thing as a "part." Quantum theory posits that we are not separated parts of a whole, but rather, *we are the Whole*. The mystical connotations of David Bohm's ideas are underlined by his statement that "the implicate domain could equally well be called Idealism, Spirit, Consciousness. The separation of the two—matter and spirit—is an abstraction. The ground is always one." Whether we look from a spiritual perspective or a scientific one, the message is the same: we are all interconnected and not separate from each other.

In terms of diversity, we must continue to acknowledge and appreciate differences while at the same time, be willing to see beyond them to the unity that connects us all. This is often difficult because we forget that we are not our egos. Our individual stories compel us, and we identify our total selves with these experiences. While our stories are real experiences, they are only a shadow of the truth.

Instead of believing that our differences and our stories are the defining qualities of who we are, we need to view them as unique aspects of our shared human experience. Recognizing that love and appreciation represent a larger truth they become instruments for working in harmony with the fundamental laws of unity, and provide the means for discovering that the essence of who we truly are is uniquely the same within us all.

When our love and appreciation become logical aspects of our problem solving strategies, our differences become a part of something larger, as do we. But we get confused, and we think that individual parts are more real than the shared and Unified Whole. When we identify ourselves by emphasizing our differences—our nation, our gender, our economic status, etc., fragmentation becomes very widespread. As we have seen, our differences are true and important, but they contain no properties of the invisible glue. **Over-emphasizing differences interferes with our clarity of perception, and prevents us from being able to solve the real human problems of disconnection, disrespect and misunderstanding.** The notion that all these different fragments are real and independent of wholeness and connection is an illusion that only leads to endless conflict and confusion. Conflicts and confusion are not going to go away, nor do we think they should, but seen only in the light of our differences they reveal no opportunity for transformation. From his book, *Wholeness and the Implicate Order*, David Bohm offers this perspective:

> *"Indeed, to some extent it has always been necessary and proper for man, in his thinking, to divide things up, if we tried to deal with the whole of reality at once, we would be swamped. However when this mode of thought is applied more broadly to man's notion of himself and the whole world in which he lives, then man ceases to regard the resultant divisions as merely useful or convenient and begins to see and experience himself and this world as actually constituted of separately existing fragments. What is needed is a relativistic theory, to give up altogether the notion that the world is constituted of basic objects or building blocks. Rather one has to view the world in terms of universal flux of events and processes."*

The following unity principles provide a foundation for the all of the key tasks and ideas in this book. These unity principles elucidate the process by which real change occurs, and give a framework for remembering *why we do want to take a risk,* leave the familiar and launch ourselves into new realms. Our lives are filled with challenges and difficulties that easily distract us from notions of unity and connectedness. Understanding and appreciating principles that underscore unity can help us to remember the power of our perceptions in creating real change, while it also helps us stay committed to being the one willing to try something new.

There is no end—there is only process

The idea of process is critically important. Yes, we may have an agenda—a specific purpose for meeting with someone. But whatever our stated reason for connecting with someone, our real job is always to simply create the energy to make a connection in the moment—which then opens the next moment differently. We cannot foresee or plan for what any moment might bring, we only need to be present and open to whatever it is that shows up.

As we approach the situations in our daily lives, we need to remember that we always have a choice about where to put our attention. Our lives are similar to a painting that we look at and discover new things in every day. Perhaps our initial impression of this painting is that of a dark and menacing landscape. And yet, by *not* turning away, and by *studying the painting more closely*, we see there is tiny flower in the corner. By noticing this small sprig of life against the darkness, we bring our attention to the potential for life and hope, and we sow the seeds of our transformation.

This potential for transformation is contained within every situation we encounter—no matter how challenging or difficult. To unlock this potential though, we need to not turn away from our own reactions. By staying connected to our own thoughts and feelings, we remain conscious of what is driving our perceptions, and this creates a choice. **We can choose to find that tiny sprig of life no matter what the circumstance, and through this learn that there is no end point—there is only ever choice, transformation and growth.** By learning to focus our attention on the process rather than on the end result, we stay connected to the field of possibilities and we begin to notice how are all things connected. Experiencing life as an ongoing flow of events that always contains opportunities for self-awareness, growth, and new choices, we begin to trust the wholeness and unity running through each of our seemingly independent lives. The richness of living in this process surpasses any notion that arriving at an end point could be as gratifying.

Possibilities exist only in the present moment

Very rarely, if ever, are we encouraged to concentrate on what is happening right now in this moment. Time is something we are trained to think about in terms of the past and the future. At different times during the next 24 hours, spend some time asking yourself, "What am I thinking about right now?" You will probably discover that you are thinking of something that happened a half an hour before, this morning, yesterday, last week. Or, you will notice that your focus is on something about to happen: a conversation you are about to have, a meeting you are not looking forward to, or an event you are looking forward to, or how you can't wait to get home. Vary rarely, if ever, are we concentrating on what is happening right now in this moment. But, of course, the past is something we cannot change, and the future is just an idea. In terms of taking action and doing something that is real, all we ever really have is right now in this moment.

In terms of diversity, however, it is important to remember the past. While we can't change the past, we need to remember it so that we don't commit the same mistakes and atrocities again. But this also presents a challenge. How do we remember the past while not being in reaction to it? It comes down to who we are in the present moment. In order to bring a new and creative future out of a painful and disturbing past, we have to be available to the possibilities that exist in the present moment by staying conscious of our reactions and our perceptions. How we choose to be in each moment is what creates our future. If we are resentful and bitter about the past, we will create a bitter and resentful future. Think how often we go back over past hurts and past anger. We replay conversations in our heads over and over, working out what we could have or should have said, recreating our anger. Every time we do this we lose energy by putting it back into a situation that is long gone, leaving it there. We need all of our energy right now in this moment, so we need to call it back. We need to ask ourselves, what are we giving our time and attention to? Am I bringing an awareness of appreciation and compassion into my experience? Do I use the present moment to find the tiny flower that brings hope and transformation into my awareness?

The present moment is where choice and action come together to generate the seeds for something creative to emerge. Choosing to be in the present moment means that we acknowledge our past, but we choose to consciously place our attention on the creative possibilities that exist only in the moment we are in. Does it mean that we never react to the past again? No. The darkness doesn't go away and neither does the past, but our conscious choice in the present moment *to be willing* to experience open-heartedness, appreciation and love changes our perception of the now, which then also changes what we do next. This is why we need to continually unlock our energy from the past and the future, and bring it into the present moment. **By shifting our perception to what we can appreciate right now, we transform our perceptions, and the present moment**

becomes the portal through which we enter into the creative field of any and all possibilities.

Every interaction is a moment of truth

In diversity terms, moments of truth are every single interaction between any two people every day. Most organisations now have diversity polices that contain fine words, ideals and principles. But diversity doesn't live and breathe in the framed mission and values statements in the reception area, in the filing cabinet, or in any of the fine words of the policy. **Diversity lives and breathes in every interaction between two people.** It doesn't matter whether it is the CEO or Managing Director talking to the waitress serving her in the dining room, the first person into the building talking to the early morning cleaners, two senior managers discussing policy, or two colleagues at the coffee machine. Our individual responsibility for diversity means that we show up in every moment to whomever we are with and pay attention to who they are in that moment. Diversity work is a constant commitment to be true to who we are and who they are.

We are all connected. What I do or say to you, ultimately, I do or say to myself. And yet our commercially oriented cultures bombard us with messages that we are all separate beings in mass competition with each other. This constant messaging leaves a mark on how we view others, and creates an unconscious tendency to see others as our competition and a threat. We are not encouraged to stop and notice all the human experiences we share with a person. Instead, we are conditioned to pay attention to all their surface characteristics and compare ourselves against them. This is where the "more than/less" scale comes in very handy. With a quick sweep based on surface characteristics, we stop looking to see who people really are. **We see them as either better than us, and we disconnect out of competition and jealousy, or we see them as less than us and disconnect out of arrogance. Either way, we lose.** Each person we meet is an opportunity to reverse this tendency. If we are willing to stay conscious and let our hearts direct our experience of a person, we will see that we are both the same. By recognizing what we have in common, we can bridge the separation in real time. This is a powerful moment. Our shared humanness is also our shared experience of the whole. We can ask ourselves, what are the human qualities that are always there between us that I can appreciate now? Through these moments of truth, we can change the kind of person we are, and the world we live in on a day-to-day basis.

Do it for yourself and you are doing it for everyone

This is an interesting principle because it reflects the process of how new ideas that were previously considered unacceptable come into mass consciousness, and the role *each person plays* in bringing about these powerful shifts in the social paradigm. History is filled with examples of what happens when an idea is introduced that threatens the prevailing worldview. For example, when Galileo maintained his position that the sun did not revolve around the earth, but that it was the other way around, he was put on house arrest for the remainder of his life. So the authorities took Galileo out of the picture, but why did the idea not go away? Why did others pursue this heretical scientific idea regardless of the menacing position of the all-powerful Church? These scientists did not yet have the "facts" to prove anything, but they clearly had a strong resonance with the idea. They were operating on a hunch. By staying committed to an idea whose time had not yet come, they helped *create the conditions* for the time to come. Grand changes in our collective view of the world do not happen overnight, but *each of us does have a role to play*—regardless of whether the change seems imminent or not. Every time we act on an idea that is true for ourselves, we keep it alive thereby increasing the possibility that this idea will be available for someone else to pick up on, and ultimately cause the unexpected events or phenomenon that ensure it reaches a critical mass. The following story of the 100th Monkey is wonderful illustration of this point. And while some have criticized the accuracy of the story, it is still a wonderful story to consider—as fact or myth—because it sheds light on the key role each individual plays in bringing about our next, unexpected leap forward. Lyall Watson first told this story in Lifetide, but its most widely known version is the opening to the book *The Hundredth Monkey*, by Ken Keyes, and is reprinted here.

The Japanese monkey, **Macaca fuscata,** had been observed in the wild for a period of over 30 years. In 1952, on the island of Koshima, scientists were providing monkeys with sweet potatoes dropped in the sand. The monkey liked the taste of the raw sweet potatoes, but they found the dirt unpleasant. An 18-month-old female named **Imo** found she could solve the problem by washing the potatoes in a nearby stream. She taught this trick to her mother. Her playmates also learned this new way and they taught their mothers too.

Various monkeys, before the eyes of the scientists, gradually picked up this cultural innovation. Between 1952 and 1958, all the young monkeys learned to wash the sandy sweet potatoes to make them more palatable. Only the adults who imitated their children learned this social improvement. Other adults kept eating the dirty sweet potatoes.

Then something startling took place. In the autumn of 1958, a certain number of **Koshima** monkeys were washing sweet potatoes—the exact number is not known. Let us suppose that when the sun rose one morning there were 99 monkeys on Koshima Island who had learned to wash their sweet potatoes. Let's further suppose that later that morning, the hundredth monkey learned to wash potatoes.

THEN IT HAPPENED! By that evening almost everyone in the tribe was washing sweet potatoes before eating them. The added energy of this hundredth monkey somehow created an ideological breakthrough!

Take notice: A most surprising thing observed by these scientists was that the habit of washing sweet potatoes then jumped over the sea…Colonies of monkeys on other islands and the mainland troop of monkeys at Takasakiyama began washing their sweet potatoes. Thus, when a certain critical number achieves an awareness, **this new awareness may be communicated from mind to mind.**

Although the exact number may vary, this **Hundredth Monkey Phenomenon** means that when only a limited number of people know of a new way, it may remain the conscious property of these people.

There is a point, when, if only one more person tunes-in to a new awareness, a field is strengthened, and this awareness is picked up by almost **everyone!**

This story demonstrates that each person needs to act on their own truth—even if they do not immediately see a direct impact on the critical mass. When we do it for ourselves, we automatically do it for those who are not yet able to. When we shift our perception to the truth that we are all connected and a part of a Unified Whole, we are holding that perception for everyone, and creating the possibility that the idea will manifest in the larger group consciousness. In an earlier chapter we saw how Andrea was able to create positive changes in her relationship with her mother by changing only *her* perception. It only takes one person to change in order to create the *possibility* for others to change. OUR doing it is enough. For example, if we truly forgive someone, we are also carrying out an act of forgiveness for all those whose hearts are still hardened and are not yet able to carry out that act. We *are* all interconnected, and in this way, we do have a direct impact on the building of the critical mass.

This story also demonstrates that no matter how powerful a new idea might be, it alone is not sufficient to create change. We still need direct communication between individuals, and each person needs to *act* on their idea—their truth-regardless of whether the idea has reached a critical mass or not. **Each person needs to stay aware of the essential role their individual actions play even if they do not immediately see a direct impact on the critical mass.**

Through the techniques in this book, you will be able to do something new: see a person differently; change your perception; move from fear to love—even if the person in front of you is not able to do the same. *You* can change things—whether they engage or not—and you can hold the space for them to walk forward and make a change until they are able to hold the space for themselves. This is a huge gift we can give to people, but we can only do it if we first create the energy inside ourselves. **You see, actually, that is all we have to offer people—our own energy of who we are in that moment.**

Do one key task and you do them all

Throughout this book, we have provided a number of key tasks. The beauty of *Creating the Energy of Connection* is that we don't need to practise these key tasks in any particular order before we start experiencing positive changes in ourselves and in our relationships with others. Actually—doing only one of the key tasks can lead to a changed dynamic between two people and a transformation in a relationship. This means that any situation is an opportunity for learning. No matter where we are, or what is in front of us, it is always an opportunity to give up an old habit and try something new. Each of the key tasks taps into the unity that underlies all of reality and re-establishes inseparability. It doesn't matter what the situation is, or what the problem involves, each time we practise any key task, we create an energetic bridge. This bridge connects us first with our own inner essence, and then extends from within ourselves to others. A person may choose to step *or not step* onto our extended bridge and the result is the same. By bridging the unity within ourselves first, we become whole and we also *become a mirror extending unity and wholeness to others.* Hopefully, many examples in this book have already illustrated how using *just one key task* can cause a huge shift in one person thereby creating a powerful shift in the relationship. In the Appendix to this book, we have included a list of all the Key Tasks and the "Let Go's," so you can try them one at a time, and in any order that you want.

We are the ones we've been waiting for

The decision to show up and be responsible for our perceptions is definitely an ongoing learning process. Many times we don't want to be the responsible one, and we just want someone to come along and do it for us. We might even have a hunch that this is a better way to resolve an issue, but we resist being the one to take the initiative and do the work to make it right. Within us all, there is a strong tendency to give in to our old patterns because they are familiar and deeply ingrained treads that provide a strong sense of predictability and control—outcomes the reptilian brain sees as the goal. We must learn to join together in a new way—a way that is not run by our old brain's collectively ingrained patterns of attack and defend. Each one of us has a key role to play. Every moment presents another chance to give up the struggle of clinging to the shore. The courage to let go and join the river is upon us now. The starting point is ourselves, and the only work to be done is our own work.

A Hopi Elder speaks

"You have been telling the people that this is the Eleventh Hour,
Now you must go back and tell the people that this is the Hour.
And there are things to be considered....
Where are you living?
What are you doing?
What are your relationships?
Are you in right relation?
Where is your water?
Know your garden.
It is time to speak your Truth.
Create your community.
Be good to each other.
And do not look outside yourself for the leader."
Then he clasped his hands together, smiled, and said,
"This could be a good time! There is a river flowing now very fast.
It is so great and swift that there are those who will be afraid.
They will try to hold on to the shore.
They will feel they are being torn apart and will suffer greatly.
Know the river has its destination.
The elders say we must let go of the shore,
Push off into the middle of the river,
Keep our eyes open, and our heads above water.
And I say, see who is in there with you and celebrate.
At this time in history, we are to take nothing personally,
Least of all ourselves, for the moment that we do,
Our spiritual growth and journey comes to a halt.
The time of the lone wolf is over.

Gather yourselves!
Banish the word struggle from your attitude and your vocabulary.
All that we do now must be done in a sacred manner and in celebration.
We are the ones we've been waiting for."

Oaibi, Arizona
Hopi Nation

APPENDIX

Summary of Key Tasks and Let Go's

Let Go's

- If something irritates us about another person surely it is our job to tell them since they are the ones who need to change

- It is impossible to love everyone so this is all ridiculous

- Not everything is a matter of opinion—some things are right and some things are wrong

- If I feel something strongly then it must be absolutely true

- Some people deserve to be punished and it's my job to do it

- You can't expect me to ditch attitudes and values I've had for years

- Even if I wanted to change—it's too hard at my age

- I know what's best for him/her/them

- There is only one way to go forward and it's my way

- Let me educate you so you will be wiser

- It's up to me to figure it out because I know more, care more and understand all the people in the situation

- We can work on connecting *after* I've told you how to change

- The world is a scary place, and I need to be worried or I won't be prepared

- It sounds like we are supposed to be robots

- If we choose to just love and accept ourselves then we are operating in complete self-delusion

- But I've still got problems and I shouldn't have should I?

Key Tasks

- Be willing to move out of denial

- Understand that by changing yourself you are changing what can happen next

- Own the world you are in—and allow others to be in their world too

- Don't be defensive

- See their behavior in their frame and not yours

- Choose compassion over judgment

- Don't try to change people—change your perception of them instead

- Have a clear statement of intent

- Work from your highest thought

- Watch your language

- See something to be grateful for in every situation

- Actively seek connections

- Listen differently

- Be open to each moment

- Ask for guidance

- Celebrate yourself—show your true colors

SUPPORTING PROGRAMMES

Supporting programmes include:

- a workbook to accompany this book for individual study

- an on-line email subscription service to download the workbook as individual monthly lessons

- a series of supporting workshops on *Creating the Energy of Connection* which will be held in the UK, in Ireland and in the US.

If you are interested in any of these support programmes, please contact us at the email addresses listed below.

Readers are invited to try out the things suggested in this book and let Mary and Geraldine know how it is working. Their next book—*Offering Ourselves Differently—How to Make it Work* will detail the examples submitted and, of course, all contributors will be acknowledged where they have given their permission.

To submit examples or find out about the supporting programmes please contact Mary or Geraldine on:

marycasey@mn.rr.com

or

geraldine@dominoperspectives.co.uk

Bibliography

Bohm, David, F. David Peat, Science, Order and Creativity, Routledge, Second Edition, 2002

Bohm David, Wholeness and Implicate Order; Routledge, 2002

Childre, Doc., Martin Howard, The HeartMath Solution, HarperSan Francisco, 1999.

Chodron, Pema, Comfortable with Uncertainty, Shambala, Boston, 2002

Chopra, Deepak, Exploring the Frontiers of Mind Body Medicine, Bantam Books, New York, 1990.

Chopra, Deepak, How to Know God: The Soul's Journey into the Mystery of Mysteries, Three Rivers Press, 2001

Damasio, A.R., Descartes' Error: Emotion, Reason and the Human Brain, Grosset/Putnam: New York, 1994).

Goleman, Daniel (Ed), Healing Emotions: Conversations with the Dalai Lama on Mindfulness, Emotions and Health; Shambala, Boston, 19997.

Handy, Charles, The Hungry Spirit: Beyond Capitalism: A Quest for Purpose in the Modern World, Broadway Books 1999.

Hawley, Jack, Reawakening the Spirit at Work; Berrett-Koehler; 1993

Mundy, Jon, Awaken to Your Own Call: Exploring a Course in Miracles; Cossroad/Herder & Herder, 1994.

Tolle, Eckhart, The Power of Now, New World Library, CA, 1999

Vanzant, Iyanla, One Day My Soul Just Opened Up : 40 Days and 40 Nights Towards Spiritual Strength and Personal Growth; Fireside, New York, 1998.

Wheatley, Margaret, Leadership and the New Science: Discovering Order in a Chaotic World, Berrett-Koehler, 1999.

Whyte, David, The Heart Aroused: Poetry and the Preservation of the Soul in Corporate America: Bantam Books, 1996.

Wilber, Ken, The Atman Project: A Transpersonal View of Human Development; Quest Books, 1996.

Williamson, Marianne, Illuminata: A Return to Prayer, Riverhead Books, 1995.

Williamson, Marianne, A Return to Love, Reflections on the Principles of "A Course in Miracles," HarperCollins, 1996.

Zohar, Danah, The Quantum Self, Human Nature and the Consciousness Defined by the New Physics, Quill/William Morrow, New York, 1990.

Printed in the United States
94018LV00006B/46-63/A